Unscripted Spirituality

Unscripted Spirituality

Making Meaning of Leadership and Faith in College

LUISA J. GALLAGHER-STEVENS

◠PICKWICK *Publications* · Eugene, Oregon

UNSCRIPTED SPIRITUALITY
Making Meaning of Leadership and Faith in College

Copyright © 2021 Luisa J. Gallagher-Stevens. All rights reserved. Except for brief quotations in critical publications or reviews, no part of this book may be reproduced in any manner without prior written permission from the publisher. Write: Permissions, Wipf and Stock Publishers, 199 W. 8th Ave., Suite 3, Eugene, OR 97401.

Pickwick Publications
An Imprint of Wipf and Stock Publishers
199 W. 8th Ave., Suite 3
Eugene, OR 97401

www.wipfandstock.com

PAPERBACK ISBN: 978-1-5326-5433-6
HARDCOVER ISBN: 978-1-5326-5434-3
EBOOK ISBN: 978-1-5326-5435-0

Cataloguing-in-Publication data:

Names: Gallagher-Stevens, Luisa J., author.
Title: Unscripted spirituality : making meaning of leadership and faith in college / Luisa J. Gallagher-Stevens.
Description: Eugene, OR : Pickwick Publications, 2020 | Includes bibliographical references.
Identifiers: ISBN 978-1-5326-5433-6 (paperback) | ISBN X978-1-5326-5434-3 (hardcover) | ISBN 978-1-5326-5435-0 (ebook)
Subjects: LCSH: College students—Religious life—United States.
Classification: LB3609 .G33 2021 (print) | LB3609 .G33 (ebook)

AUGUST 9, 2021

All Scripture quotations, unless otherwise indicated, are taken from the Holy Bible, New International Version®, NIV®. Copyright ©1973, 1978, 1984, 2011 by Biblica, Inc.™ Used by permission of Zondervan. All rights reserved worldwide. www.zondervan.com The "NIV" and "New International Version" are trademarks registered in the United States Patent and Trademark Office by Biblica, Inc.™

This book is dedicated to my sister, Sarita Gallagher Edwards,
and to my parents, Robert and Dolores Gallagher,
who gave me the love and encouragement
to pursue Christ in all things.

Contents

Acknowledgments | ix

1 Introduction—Listening to Students' Spiritual Stories | 1
2 Approaches to Christian Spiritual Formation | 16
3 The Importance of Faith Conversations | 28
4 The Development of Spiritual Identity | 43
5 The Development of Leadership Identity | 60
6 The Role of Transitions and Suffering | 80
7 The Path toward Spiritual Resilience | 99
8 The Emergence of Spiritual and Leadership Congruence | 108
9 Conclusion—Supporting Emerging Adults in College | 125

Bibliography | 135

Acknowledgments

I WOULD LIKE TO thank my sister, Dr. Sarita D. Gallagher Edwards, and father, Dr. Robert L. Gallagher, for their continued encouragement throughout the research and writing process, and their assistance in reading and giving feedback on this book.

This book is possible with the generous support of the M. J. Murdock Charitable Trust. I appreciate the hospitality and care you showed during my time as a visiting scholar with the Trust.

I would also like to acknowledge the assistance of my dissertation chair, Dr. JoAnn Barbour, and dissertation committee members, Dr. David Setran and Dr. Shann Ferch. Thank you for your time and energy, and excellent feedback throughout the writing stages of my study.

I am grateful to Gonzaga University for allowing me to conduct my research on their campus and interview student leaders. Particularly, I am thankful for the Gonzaga student leaders that participated in this study and shared so openly. You all inspire me, and are the reason this study has meaning.

1

Introduction
Listening to Students' Spiritual Stories

WHEN SPIRITUALITY IS MENTIONED, one might conjure up images of a guru sitting on a mountaintop, or a devout religious follower, such as a priest or pastor. Mother Teresa, the Dalai Lama, or Mahatma Ghandi may come to mind when discussing spirituality and leadership, but perhaps not a twenty-year-old undergraduate student. Although spiritual language is often unscripted in nature, emerging adults, ages seventeen to twenty-three, continue to seek opportunities to express their beliefs, faith, religion, and spiritual life in their educational experiences. In this book, the interplay of spirituality and leadership is explored via the spiritual narratives of undergraduate Catholic and Protestant student leaders at Gonzaga, a Jesuit, Catholic, humanist liberal arts university.

Spirituality can take many different expressions, from organized religion and personal faith, to a reflective and meditative form, including yoga and private prayer. In academic circles, the term spiritual formation, or spiritual development, is used interchangeably to express growth and one's ability to clarify values, enact new expressions of faith, and make meaning of her or his life. Spirituality can function as an internal disposition as well as a framework that orients people to their place in the world and gives them motivation for life. I will unwrap the commonly held definition of spirituality in academia and clarify the definition of spirituality to be used in this study that is rooted in scholarship.

In academic research, spirituality is expressed as an individual's ability to explore life's big questions, and to live out one's convictions and ideals. Parks explained that for young adults, "making meaning includes (1) becoming critically aware of one's own composing of reality, (2) self-conscientiously participating in an ongoing dialogue toward truth, and (3) cultivating a capacity to respond—to act—in ways that are satisfying and just."[1] According to Astin and coauthors, the comprehensive definition of spiritual formation can be explained in terms of purpose and values, as well as the inclusion of faith, religion and the mystical elements of students' lives. Astin and coauthors define spirituality as a (1) spiritual quest, as students seek self-awareness and answers to big life questions; (2) equanimity, as students find meaning in hardship; (3) charitable involvement, or service; (4) ethic of caring, or a commitment to helping others and reducing suffering; and, finally, (5) ecumenical worldview, as students seek to understand others, and find a connection to all humanity.[2] For students, spirituality can give clarity, and a greater sense of self, helping the student toward self-authorship.

Spirituality is considered more than just a religious tradition, but as a way to make meaning from life and to align values, which are important to many atheists as well. Chickering and coauthors posited that just as religious individuals, many atheists "share a contemplative attitude, a disposition to a life of depth, and the search for ultimate meaning, direction, and belonging and are committed to growth."[3] Spirituality is an important dimension in students' holistic education at university; it promotes diversity of thought, personal growth, as well as mental, emotional, and

---

1. Parks, *Big Questions, Worthy Dreams*, 6.
2. Astin et al., *Cultivating the Spirit*, 20–21.
3. Chickering et al., *Encouraging Authenticity and Spirituality*, 8.

Introduction

physical health.[4] There are many forms of holistic spiritual practices that can benefit all students, from meditation, prayer, and time in nature, nutrition, sleep and stress-relieving exercise. Dugan and Komives suggest, "Increases in leadership development in turn enhance the self-efficacy, civic engagement, character development, academic performance, and personal development of students."[5] The overlap of leadership and spiritual identity formation will be explored in this book. Both elements of spiritual and leadership identity formation are developed during an individual's lifetime and particularly during college, where student leaders observe leadership and spirituality modeled by adult figures, and have opportunities to explore and practice both spirituality and leadership.

This book is based on research I conducted among student leaders from unique faith and spiritual backgrounds, some participants were raised in families with strong nonreligious values, while others were raised as "cradle Catholics" and cannot imagine a time in their life without religious or faith influences. These participants will be described in greater detail in the section "Spiritual Stories." In this book, I looked to students to help define spirituality. In expressing differences between spirituality and faith or religion, the participants varied in understanding and definition. A student in the study noted, "For me, spirituality and faith they are basically the same thing,"[6] and another student concurred that her spirituality "really does have a tie to my faith."[7] An additional student commented, "Spirituality I don't think needs to pertain to Christian faith, but for me that is important . . . with the . . . Spirit [of God] . . . at the center of you and your being."[8] Another student explained her faith and spirituality as distinct, but "interwoven."[9]

---

4. Astin et al., *Cultivating the Spirit*; Chickering et al., *Encouraging Authenticity and Spirituality*; Light, *Making the Most of College*.
5. Dugan and Komives, *Developing Leadership Capacity*, 8.
6. Johnson, focus group interview, November 4, 2016.
7. Amir, focus group interview, November 4, 2016.
8. Jones, focus group interview, November 3, 2016.
9. Gray, focus group interview, November 4, 2016.

Therefore for the remainder of the student discussion on spiritual identity, faith and spiritual identity will be used interchangeably.

Similar to spirituality, leadership can include many different elements, thereby making it difficult to define. "There are almost as many definitions of leadership as there are people who have attempted to describe the concept."[10] The process of defining leadership is connected to the concept of social constructivism. Woodward and coauthors suggest, "Views of leadership have changed over time as society and relationships have changed."[11] Yukl likewise noted the challenges of shifting perspectives, "Leadership means different things to different people."[12] According to social constructivism, knowledge, or meaning is socially constructed through human interaction and activity.[13] In other words, society is not merely an environmental context, but social life shapes and influences how we make meaning. Bennis exclaimed, "Leadership is like beauty: it's hard to define, but you know it when you see it."[14]

Early scholars focused on leaders as key figures in leadership theory, while some scholars have emphasized the important role of followers, and more recently, process and collaboration have been influential concepts in leadership theory. Koestenbaum, described leadership as prescriptive, rather than descriptive, noting a philosophical analysis: "We live in a common world; we all have needs and hopes, feelings and ideals. We ask, 'What kind of people does it take to achieve these goals?' And, more important, 'What kind of people does it take to help others achieve them, to create environments and societies—durable ones, sustainable ones—that will facilitate these goals?'"[15] Leadership has been described as the influence between a leader and collaborators or followers toward a common goal.

10. Stogdill, *Handbook of Leadership*, 259.
11. Woodward et al., "Leadership," 83.
12. Yukl, *Leadership in Organizations*, 2.
13. Vygotsky, *Mind in Society*.
14. Bennis, *On Becoming a Leader*, 1.
15. Koestenbaum, *Leadership*, xiii.

Across college student leadership research and theory there is a common theme of defining leadership, not as a positional, or managerial approach, but rather a reciprocal and relational model. Komives and coauthors noted, "Socially responsible leaders are concerned about the well-being of group members and about the impact of the group's decisions on the community."[16]

To make sense of various terminologies and practices, I narrow and focus the definition of spirituality by combining both current academic explanations and traditional Christian spiritual formation texts from the Jesuit Roman Catholic and Wesleyan Protestant traditions. Spirituality in this study is expressed as the action and reflection of the Christian faith that Ignatius of Loyola promoted, an inward journey and outward expression of faith, along with cognitive thinking, as explained by John Wesley. The leadership definition to be used, is based on the servant role of a servant leadership, along with the Leadership Identity Development model. Considering the potential impact of spirituality on individuals, community, and culture, higher education has an important role to play in the development of the education of undergraduate students.

Listening to Students' Spiritual Stories

For the past twelve years, I have worked in higher education in the field of student development and currently teach in university settings with traditional-aged college students and also graduate students. My time in higher education has been spent at a large research university in Australia and at four private faith-based liberal arts universities in the United States, both Protestant and Catholic. I currently teach at a seminary in Portland, Oregon, and most recently served as a minister at a small nondenominational Protestant church community in Portland, Oregon. My theological background is of the Wesleyan tradition, which contends that faith and theology affect all aspects of life, including learning and

---

16. Komives and Wagner, *Leadership for a Better World*, 33.

scholarship, engagement in the faith and local community, and sharing the good news about Christ. Through my various leadership roles, I have lived with, supervised, and engaged in transformational work with students, particularly student leaders. As a spiritual leader in my community and as an educator, I have become increasingly interested in how a university education can develop the whole person, particularly through spiritual formation, and the possible leadership outcomes of such intentional reflection.

Many universities either fail to see the importance of holistic and spiritual education, or they find themselves torn between competing priorities of staying financially viable, and relevant, training students for skill acquisition, and eventual employment. In higher education today it can be difficult to have the longer view. With the dichotomy of educational purposes in mind, I sought to hear directly from students. Spiritual narratives can provide educators with useful, rich data to adapt curriculum and cocurricular learning to best educate whole students.

The goal of this book is to tell the spiritual stories of student leaders from the students' voice and to draw themes and insights from the range of group and individual interviews. In conducting research for this book, I asked the following overarching questions: (1) What are students' spiritual experiences during college? (2) How do student leaders make meaning in their lives from spiritual experiences? And, (3) What impact do spiritual experiences have, if any, on students' leadership identity?

In this study, I used both in-depth one-on-one interviews and focus groups. The total participant pool included fourteen undergraduate students, split between the two focus groups over a two-day period. Focus groups were comprised of six to eight students, male and female, from different leadership positions on campus. The focus groups gave insight into student context and perspective, and gave the possibility to raise questions for follow up in the second stage of research: the student interview. Students involved in this study self-identified as either Protestant or Catholic, considered themselves to be spiritual, and spent at least two

Introduction

years at Gonzaga. The sample population of college student leaders that are emerging adults ages seventeen to twenty-three provided a distinct and narrow demographic to study.

From this same pool of fourteen total students, I invited eight individuals to participate in a one-on-one interview conducted the following week. I conducted the two focus groups in a one-week period, and held eight one-on-one interviews the following week over a four-day period. In the focus group interviews, I used structured questions, while the questions used during the interviews were open-ended, allowing students to construct their responses with as little interference or leading from myself as a researcher. Those students indicating that spirituality was "extremely important" to her or him were asked to participate in individual interviews.

In this study, I used snowball sampling, a non-probability sampling method to select participants. The method of snowball sampling is similar to advertising by word of mouth in a university environment and provided the best results for gathering an adequate sample population. The initial group of students invited to participate in turn were asked to reach out to other students they know or believe to be spiritual and meet the criteria. I also used purposive recruitment, and contacted university student leadership staff and faculty advisors asking for recommendations of hired or volunteer student leaders to participate in the study.

Following the email to Gonzaga student leaders, I received interest from over twenty-five student leaders. The demographic form I created from the online survey data indicated that of those twenty-five, five students did not meet the study requirements as they identified as sophomores, or did not profess to be Protestant or Catholic, or had left the Christian faith. I eventually had twenty student leaders interested in participating in the study, and after cancellations, scheduling conflict, or when students forgot to show up to the interview, fourteen students remained to participate in the study. Students who met the criteria for this study filled out a demographic survey providing background information such as gender, age, amount of time at Gonzaga, faith background, and volunteer or hired leadership position.

For this particular study on spirituality and leadership, I use a qualitative research approach. Qualitative research is an exploratory and interactive process, intended to uncover trends in thinking and feelings surrounding a topic, while involving both researcher and participant in making new meaning. In contrast, quantitative research tends toward objective data and results, and testing of a hypothesis.

Quantitative approaches tend to be popular in the field of spiritual research, and often allows for larger scale projects through the utilization of surveys and Likert scales. The field of spirituality research has a large amount of quantitative data from the study conducted by the Higher Education Research Institute (HERI) out of their office at the University of California Los Angeles (UCLA).[17] During their research, they surveyed 112,000 first-year students in 236 universities and followed up with 14,527 of these students after their junior year at 136 colleges.[18] Their seminal work continues to remain pertinent in the field of spiritual study. Shahabi and coauthors conducted a survey in 1998 with 1,422 adult American respondents on the correlates of self-perception of spirituality.[19] Benson, Donahue, and Erickson used a quantitative 38-item 7-point Likert survey to achieve empirical validation of the faith maturity scale.[20] They conducted research with over 11,000 adolescents and adults from six different Protestant denominations. Wood and Hebert also used a survey to assess the relationship between spiritual meaning and purpose and drug and alcohol use among college students.[21] Their sample population included 606 undergraduate students. Berry and York conducted a longitudinal quantitative study assessing the effect of spirituality on depression in 214 college students from religious and public

17. Astin et al., *Cultivating the Spirit*.
18. Astin et al., *Cultivating the Spirit*.
19. Shahabi et al., "Correlates of Self-Perception of Spirituality."
20. Benson et al., "Faith Maturity Scale."
21. Wood and Hebert, *Relationship between Spiritual Meaning and Purpose*.

colleges.[22] Such quantitative research provides a good framework for generalizable data, while qualitative research provides a deeper dive into the lives and meaning making on topics that require in-depth reflection and conversation.

Spirituality is making meaning from lived experiences, so the process of exploring spirituality is purposefully addressed in this study through a qualitative constructivist approach of narrative inquiry. Social constructivists believe that individuals create meaning through their interactions with each other and with the environment they live in, shaping constructions of consciousness, knowledge, learning, reality or perception. Social meanings, symbols, language and knowledge are shaped and evolve through negotiation within communicating groups. Each participant has a distinct and unique perspective, and the categories and themes that are used to make meaning of the interviews emerged from the interviews and the data itself. As a researcher undertaking a constructivist, qualitative study, I am not seeking the "truth" of spirituality, but the perception, understanding, and experience of spirituality in the lives of undergraduate student leaders.

Through narrative inquiry of student's leadership and spiritual life experiences, this text reveals unique insights into the perspectives of undergraduate student leaders as they face difficult life challenges, have intimate encounters with God, and explore their leadership identity. The interviews and focus group conversations were transcribed verbatim from each with minor edits not including nonessential or repetitive words such as "like" and "um." To maintain participant anonymity I used pseudonyms to express student experiences and stories.

Using narrative analysis, I analyzed, coded, and interpreted the focus group and interview text transcribed, capturing the essence of the undergraduate students and their spiritual narratives. I personally coded and hand-analyzed the transcripts from the two focus groups and eight interviews. In the analysis of the focus groups and one-on-one interviews, I considered the influence of cultural and social context, and the structure and themes that can

22. Berry and York, "Depression and Religiosity."

emerge over multiple narratives. To analyze this data, I utilized thematic analysis by looking for overlapping themes and significance in the spiritual narratives. This thematic method of analysis displayed the rich layers that can be revealed through story. I tied threads together that describe a "thick description"[23] of spirituality among the stories of positional student leaders at Gonzaga University. Reading through the transcripts multiple times, I created codes for initial concepts that appear, and further summarize multiple codes that overlap and have significant similarities.

In the interpretation of the findings from the spiritual narratives, I looked for the overlap of the spiritual formation model (see figure 2), the Leadership Identity Development (LID) theoretical framework and the characteristics of servant leadership as outlined by Larry Spears. The LID model was the main driving leadership theory, while servant leadership provided a definitional component of leadership for this study. Many of the student leaders at Gonzaga University have received training in servant leadership; therefore, it was interesting to review their understanding of leadership and how it connected to their spirituality. While at Gonzaga, these same students were situated in a larger context of Jesuit, humanist education.

A Jesuit University Context

A hallmark of Jesuit education includes an emphasis on the development of the whole person, or, the formation of "women and men for others."[24] Gonzaga University is one such school in the Jesuit tradition: a private, liberal arts university in Spokane, Washington, in the northwestern part of the state. The 152-acre campus is located a half-mile from downtown Spokane and is situated along the picturesque Spokane River.[25] Gonzaga University is a coeducational university with masters, undergraduate, and doctoral

23. Geertz, *Interpretation of Cultures*, 3.
24. ICAJE, "Ignatian Pedagogy," 241.
25. Gonzaga University, "At a Glance" (2015).

programs, as well as a law school. The school was originally established in 1887. In 2015 when I conducted these interviews, there were 5,041 full-time undergraduate students at Gonzaga; 72 percent of the students were "white," and 20 percent signified race as "other," with the second largest ethnicity documented as 10 percent "Hispanic," and third largest percentage of 5 percent self-identifying as "Asian."[26] Of the undergraduate student population, 54 percent of the population is female and 46 percent male.[27] The top five undergraduate degrees the university awards are ranked in order: business, social sciences, engineering, psychology, and biological/life sciences.[28]

Gonzaga's administrators note the importance of spiritual and faith formation to the stakeholders at the university. According to the strategic plan, families "see tremendous value in cura personalis—the care of the entire person."[29] It is the desire of Gonzaga University that its students would see and recognize God in all aspects of life, from a walk across campus, to being grateful for a sense of peace in the middle of an exam. Former Vice President of Mission Frank E. Case, SJ, commented, "A cornerstone of Ignatian Spirituality is this idea of finding God in all things. Since God is present in all things, however, it is not so much a matter of searching for God as of seeing and recognizing God."[30]

Gonzaga is a Jesuit, humanist, Catholic liberal arts university intentionally residential and community-minded, with 60 percent of students living in university owned or affiliated housing each year. In the residence halls, Gonzaga students also have a Jesuit priest living in many of the buildings. The university attracts many students because of its participation and success in men's basketball in the NCAA. As noted by Herak, trustee emeritus and major

26. Gonzaga University, "Common Data Set 2015–2016," 5; Gonzaga University, "Undergraduate Student Body Diversity," para. 1.
27. Gonzaga University, "Common Data Set 2015–2016," 5.
28. Gonzaga University, "Common Data Set 2015–2016," 38.
29. ICAJE, "Characteristics of Jesuit Education," 181; Gonzaga University, "Strategic Plan," 2.
30. Case, "Finding God in All Things," 47.

Unscripted Spirituality

donor, "Gonzaga was really suffering [in 1999], the basketball team was the catalyst for changing Gonzaga" in terms of enrollment, donations, and nationwide branding.[31] While at the university, students can participate in a number of religious and spiritual, academic, and cocurricular activities.

The requirement of the core curriculum for students prior to the summer of 2016, those participating in this study, lists religious studies for nine credits: scriptural studies, Christian doctrine, and applied theology.[32] Jesuit education intends to form students morally and prepare them for active participation in society through service. The university lists over 142,000 hours of students serving in the community and has recently acquired the prestigious Carnegie classification for community engagement.[33] There are 811 total staff employed at Gonzaga University, with 427 full-time staff members and 384 part-time staff members.[34] Spiritual experts at the university consist largely of the Jesuit priests living on campus, the office of Mission, and the staff at the office of University Ministry. There are twenty-three Jesuits listed on the Jesuit community page on Gonzaga's website.[35] According to Mark Raper, SJ, the numbers of Jesuits entering the priesthood "have been in decline for the last 40 years—from over 30,000 in the 1960s to fewer than 18,000 today."[36] At the school's founding, Gonzaga had seventeen Jesuits at the campus, with a strong Jesuit-to-student ratio of nearly 1:1, and in 2013 there were thirty-one Jesuits connected to the campus, and fewer still involved in the day-to-day student experience, leaving a ratio of 156 students to 1 Jesuit faculty or staff.[37] In 2016 the number of Jesuits dropped to just twenty-two Jesuits working with students on the Gonzaga campus.[38]

31. Lawrence-Turner, "Gonzaga University's Basketball Success," para. 6.
32. Gonzaga University, "Degree Requirements."
33. Gonzaga University, "At a Glance" (2015).
34. Gonzaga University, "At a Glance" (2015).
35. Gonzaga University, "Meet the Jesuits" (2015).
36. Raper, "Changing to Best Serve the Universal Mission," para. 2.
37. Plowman, "Gonzaga History."
38. Gonzaga University, "Meet the Jesuits" (2016).

Introduction

Situated in the administrative building in the center of campus, the student chapel is available to students twenty-four hours a day. The student chapel also provides a meeting space for students to gather for mass each Sunday night during the school year. Students also have access to chapels in many of the residence halls, and a place of reflection now included in the newly built student center, the John H. Hemmingson Center. If invited, students can attend luncheon at the Jesuit house, and are able to visit the Jesuit house chapel if interested. Students can join Christian Life Community groups, over sixteen spiritual retreats, and spiritual direction during the school year at University Ministry, participate in service activities through the Center for Community Action and Social Change, as well as service opportunities through academic departments.[39] Student groups such as Thirst also provide an opportunity for Protestant and Catholic students to worship together mid-week.

Significance of the Study

In this study, I focus on one university in a particular time and place, influenced by a specific Jesuit, Catholic context. Gonzaga University offers a good example of similar institutions in the United States that are faced with a lowering of staff, faculty and administration trained in the areas of spiritual formation. The traditional-aged undergraduate population likewise provides a narrow sampling of student populations in the United States. An additional delimitation of the study is the homogenous pool of student leaders and the use of Protestant and Catholic Christian student leaders faith background, indicating spirituality as "important," "fairly important," or "extremely important" to the student. Instead of focusing on generalizability of results, narrative inquiry shines in the layering of similar studies, and the overlap of patterns of similarity and difference. In this study, the students led the direction of the study through their spiritual narratives,

---

39. Gonzaga University, "At a Glance" (2015).

indicating what mattered in their perspectives in terms of spirituality, religion, and leadership.

This study holds significance for academia by adding to the current research of spirituality in the lives of undergraduate students. Despite the growing interest in spiritual formation in higher education, very few researchers have looked at the overlap of leadership identity and spirituality in academic research, and there has been no exploration of spiritual development in students through the lens of the spiritual formation model found in figure 2. The Catholic, Jesuit University approach to spiritual formation and context of Gonzaga provides a unique perspective, and the introduction of the overlap of leadership, along with the spiritual formation model in figure 2 offers a unique research perspective. It is my intent to fill the gap left by the research already conducted in health sciences, graduate programs, church and religious behavior, diversity, self-authorship and identity.

Outline of the Book

Chapters 1 and 2 provide an overview for the book and the basis of my research. Chapter 2 explains multiple approaches to Christian spiritual formation, describing the Jesuit and Wesleyan spiritual traditions of experiential and transformative faith pedagogies. I also explore a Wesleyan-Ignatian Pedagogical model, explaining a new approach to spiritual formation.

The following chapters highlight themes that emerged from student's spiritual stories. Based on the interviews and focus group discussions, I use student's quotes about their spiritual stories to explore those themes.

Chapter 3 reviews the importance of faith conversations in spiritual development, and the key role of parents and mentors in engaging with young adults around faith topics. Such conversations can create greater confidence and stability as students figure out what they believe, and how they can apply their beliefs and values to their lives.

Introduction

Chapter 4 continues the conversation around spiritual identity development, noting the role of transitions in spiritual growth. College is a time of great exploration, where students are often forced into new environments and exposed to new belief systems, in this chapter I consider how such exposure impacts students' spirituality and formation. In chapter 4, I also review the importance of spiritual experience in students' faith ownership.

Chapter 5 examines the Leadership Identity Development (LID) theory, and the factors impacting student leaders' formation. I also review what students value in leadership settings, from authentic and vulnerable leadership styles, to characteristics from servant leadership such as listening and the desire to serve.

Chapter 6 considers the role of transitions during college as a form of suffering. Students must process some small and great challenges during college, from leaving family and communities, many for the first time, to dealing with family sickness and newfound responsibility. Transitions of college life can often unsettle students' equilibrium as relationships change and shift and are formed and reformed. Yet, in the midst of these often difficult transitions, students mention the sustaining work of the Holy Spirit.

Chapter 7 considers the path students take toward spiritual resilience, often including a familiarity with one's own story. Other factors of developing spiritual resilience include the student's ability to ask for help and spiritual practices of self-care.

Chapter 8 describes students' grappling with spiritual and leadership congruence. In this chapter, students explain the importance of both relational spirituality and relational leadership approaches, noting that in caring for those they lead, individuals are doing spiritual and relational work.

Chapter 9 summarizes concluding thoughts, explaining how parents, college faculty and staff, religious leaders, and mentors can best support students in college. It is my hope that the spiritual and leadership stories and themes of these student leaders can present helpful insights into the spiritual and leadership lives of college students and assist those working with students in providing ample support as they navigate their college years.

2

Approaches to Christian Spiritual Formation

HIGHER EDUCATION TODAY REQUIRES a holistic and ecumenical approach to spiritual formation. This chapter explores the complementary nature of the Jesuit and Wesleyan understanding of spirituality and provides a contextual example of an integrated Wesleyan-Ignatian model of spiritual formation among undergraduate students in higher education.

The pedagogy of education at a Jesuit university is based on the biblical tenants of the Catholic faith, and the Jesuit pedagogy of context, experience, reflection, action, and evaluation. Ignatius of Loyola, the founder of the Society of Jesus, also called Jesuits, advocated for a lifestyle of spirituality, leadership, and intellectual rigor. Jesuit, or Ignatian education is a holistic and interactive formation process that seeks to "accompany the learner in their growth and development."[1] The Jesuits are often called contemplatives in action, focusing on action and reflection in spiritual development. Ignatian educational imperatives often emphasize the experiential dynamics of spiritual formation, including the use of imagination, story, and a desire to see God in all things.

---

1. Duminuco, *Jesuit Ratio*, 240, no. 11.

Approaches to Christian Spiritual Formation

The combined emphasis of Ignatian reflection and action along with Jesuit pedagogy is mirrored in the thinking of many Christian writers, and educators. John Wesley, a Christian theologian, author, and pastor, sought to engage Christians in faith development as an experiential combination of head, heart, and hands. Wesley emphasized the importance of faith with works, describing spiritual engagement as a *means of grace*, or a sanctifying movement toward Christlikeness.[2] The Wesleyan and Jesuit experiential spiritual dynamics of heart (reflection), and hands (action) are complementary, while the disproportionate focus on the head (reason, or cognitive thinking) continues to be the focus of much of faith formation in evangelical higher education, seminary, churches and parishes.[3]

In the following sections, Ignatian and Wesleyan philosophies of Christian spiritual formation are explored. Additionally, a Wesleyan-Ignatian spiritual formation model is presented which focuses on engaging the whole person in cognitive theological thinking, inward spiritual journey, and an outward expression of faith and service.

Ignatian Pedagogy: An Experiential Faith

In the Jesuit tradition, experiential activity is coupled with reflection to develop meaning from action. Similar to the spiritual exercises of the Jesuit founder, Ignatius of Loyola, Ignatian pedagogy emphasizes that the "whole person—mind, heart and will—should enter the learning experience."[4] In Ignatian education and learning "participants must attend to and recollect the *experience* of the day fully, then they must *reflect* on that experience, to formulate a course of *action*, which they can later *evaluate*."[5] The Jesuit pedagogy listed in figure 1 is a continuous cycle, beginning with the

2. Wesley, "Sermon 16."

3. Wilhoit et al., "Soul Projects," 153–78; Willard, "Transformation of the Mind."

4. ICAJE, "Ignatian Pedagogy," 254.

5. Nowacek and Mountin, "Reflection in Action," 134.

concept of *context*, proceeding through each stage clockwise, before entering back into the learning experience.

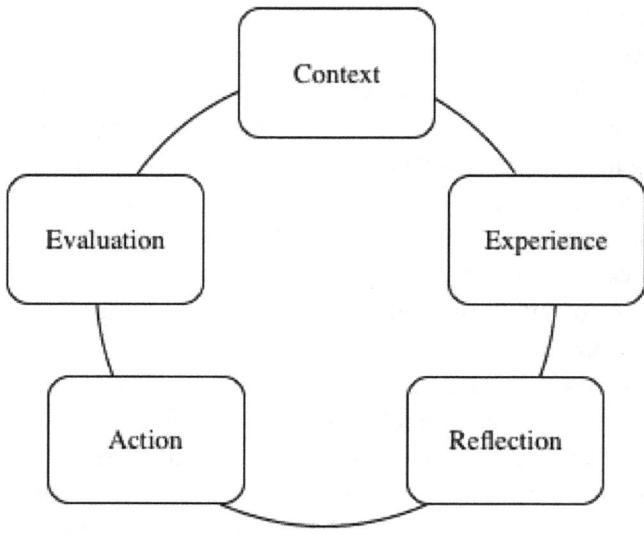

Figure 1. Jesuit pedagogy.

An example of *context* in the *Spiritual Exercises* utilized by Ignatius and the Society of Jesus, encourages the spiritual director to "adapt to the condition of the one who is to engage."[6] *Context* includes "the socioeconomic, political and cultural context within which a student grows . . . the institutional environment of the school or learning center . . . and previously acquired concepts students bring with them to the start of the learning process."[7] Following *context*, in Ignatian spiritual formation, *reflection* means "a thoughtful reconsideration of some subject matter, experience, idea, purpose or spontaneous reaction, to grasp its significance more fully . . . the process by which meaning surfaces in human experience."[8] The

6. Ignatius of Loyola and Puhl, *Spiritual Exercises*, 7.
7. ICAJE, "Ignatian Pedagogy," 253–54.
8. ICAJE, "Ignatian Pedagogy," 257.

Approaches to Christian Spiritual Formation

hope of Jesuit spiritual formation is that individuals would move from reflection toward meaningful action.

Action is the goal of the learning process, to move individuals to engage with new knowledge they have experienced and appropriated. *Action* refers to "internal human growth based upon experience that has been reflected upon as well as to its manifestation externally."[9] *Action* is a two-step process, involving the interior, such as a shift in attitude, or perspective, and external choices, such as a physical action "to do something consistent with this new conviction."[10] Jesuit *action* is mirrored in the Greek term *phroneō*, found in Philippians 2:5–6, which notes that the Christian's attitude should be "in the same mind as Christ," "who being in very nature God, did not consider equality with God something to be used to his own advantage." Following *context, experience, reflection*, and *action*, the final stage requires learners and educators to evaluate the process, adapt, and then actively enter back into the process of learning. In spiritual terms, reflection can be a tool for undergraduate students to gain insight, wisdom and greater understanding of self and others.

In Jesuit spirituality, educators are looking not only to influence individuals, but also to create leaders who will influence the world for the common good. Duminuco writes, "If truly successful, Jesuit education results ultimately in a radical transformation not only of the way in which people habitually *think* and act, but of the very way in which they live in the world, men and women of competence, conscience and compassion, seeking the *greater good* in terms of what can be done out of a faith commitment with justice to enhance the quality of peoples' lives, particularly among the poor, oppressed and neglected."[11] Ignatian education is not just intended as a method for learning information, but rather, as a transformational way of proceeding in the world.

---

9. ICAJE, "Ignatian Pedagogy," 260.
10. ICAJE, "Ignatian Pedagogy," 261.
11. ICAJE, "Ignatian Pedagogy," 243.

Wesleyan Pedagogy: A Transformed Life

Spiritual formation is viewed by Wesley and Ignatius as an inner transformation of the heart that outwardly expresses its faith and belief. Wesley noted that he was less concerned that the Methodist church would continue to exist after his death than he was about developing in Christian believers a living and active faith reliant on Christ.[12] Rather, he explained his fear that Methodists would "exist as a dead sect, having the form of religion without the power. And this undoubtedly will be the case, unless they hold fast both the doctrine, spirit and discipline with which they first set out."[13] Considering Wesley's desire for transformed lives among Methodist believers, and paired with a rich cognitive Scriptural engagement, Wesley approached Christian spiritual formation and discipleship experientially, engaging the whole person in areas of faith and works.

Wesley, drew his understanding of Christian spiritual formation from his personal encounter with God at Aldersgate. Although already having an intellectual knowledge of God, Wesley's experience with the Holy Spirit at Aldersgate Street in London dramatically shifted his prior understanding of faith and his life with God. In his journal on May 24, 1738, he wrote, "I felt my heart strangely warmed. I felt I did trust in Christ, Christ alone for salvation: And an assurance was given me, that he had taken away my sins, even mine, and saved me from the law of sin and death."[14] Wesley's followers, first mocked for their "holy" living and method of pursuing Christian perfection, eventually took the name of Methodist. Methodists engaged regularly in societies and classes that met weekly to pray and read Scripture.

In explaining Christian spiritual formation and discipleship, Wesley signified that spiritual actions, words, or signs serve as *means of grace* that sanctify the Christian follower toward

---

12. Wesley, "Thoughts upon Methodism," in *Works*, 7:315.
13. Wesley, "Thoughts upon Methodism," in *Works*, 7:315.
14. Quoted in Dean, *Heart Strangely Warmed*, 36.

Christlikeness.[15] These means of grace are distinguished by works of piety, including meditating on and reading Scripture, prayer, fasting, worship, sharing of faith with others, and communal practices such as taking the sacraments. For Wesley, means of grace also include works of mercy such as visiting the poor and sick, and those in prison, feeding the hungry, and ending oppression and injustice. Wesley noted the most important means of grace "are prayer . . . searching the Scriptures; (which implies reading, hearing, and meditating thereon); and receiving the Lord's Supper."[16] Scripture played a central role in Wesley's theology, supported by reason, experience, and tradition.[17] In describing means of grace, Wesley acknowledged that Christians cannot earn God's mercy, and without God, spiritual works are dead and empty. Instead, he suggested, "in using all means, seek God alone. In and through every outward thing, look singly to the power of his Spirit; and the merits of his Son. . . . Nothing short of God can satisfy your soul."[18]

Wesleyan-Ignatian Pedagogy: A New Approach to Spiritual Formation

The spiritual formation model (see figure 2) is mirrored in Christian theology, including the head, heart, and hands model of spiritual growth of Wesley, in Jesuit educational imperatives, and contemporary spiritual writing.[19] This holistic approach draws on Christ's command to "love the Lord your God with all your heart, and with all your soul, and with all your mind," and to "love your neighbor as yourself."[20] The Matthew 22:36–39 passage looks to the congruence and integrity of faith with praxis. The following

15. Wesley, "Sermon 16."
16. Wesley, "Sermon 16," 152.
17. Outler, "Wesleyan Quadrilateral."
18. Wesley, "Sermon 16," 162.
19. Hollinger, *Head, Heart and Hands*; Nouwen, *Way of the Heart*.
20. Matt 22:36–39.

spiritual formation model is adapted from King and Magolda's[21] take on Kegan's lifespan developmental model,[22] and Braskamp, Doyle, and Zylstra's Global Perspective Inventory.[23] The Global Perspective Inventory is designed to measure student growth in global learning, answering the questions of "how do I know," "who am I," and "how do I relate to others?"[24] The model follows a similar overlap of spiritual transformation and learning between cognitive thinking, intrapersonal inward journey, and interpersonal outward expression.

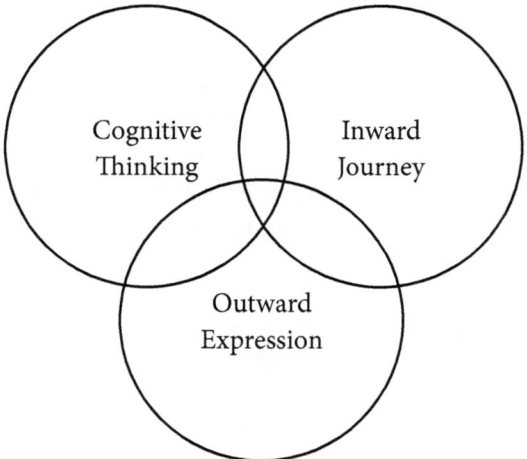

Figure 2. Spiritual formation model.

Christian spiritual formation emphasizes inner transformation, where transformative cognitive thinking happens when someone changes "not just what he knows but the way he knows."[25] The Apostle Paul admonishes Christians to "have the same mindset as Christ,"[26] and he encourages followers of Christ to "not conform to the pattern of this world, but be transformed by the renewing

21. King and Magolda, "Developmental Model of Intercultural Maturity."
22. Kegan, *In Over Our Heads*.
23. Braskamp et al., "Using the Global Perspective Inventory."
24. Braskamp et al., "Using the Global Perspective Inventory."
25. Kegan, *In Over Our Heads*, 17.
26. Phil 2:5.

Approaches to Christian Spiritual Formation

of your mind," for "then you will be able to test and approve what God's will is—his good, pleasing and perfect will."[27]

The Jesuit approach to cognitive knowledge implies that knowing God is more valuable that merely knowing about God. It is in knowing Christ that the person understands more about God, for Christ embodied God.[28] Martin articulates the role of Scripture as a guide to knowing God. He notes, "Reading Scripture helps to inspire us, in the literal sense of the word-placing God's spirit into us. . . . In Scripture you see God relating to you, to humanity and to individuals. In all these ways Scripture helps you to come to know God better."[29] Ignatian spirituality is not merely the accumulation of information, but a transforming, relational, practical encounter with the living God.

For Wesley, Scripture and reason play complementary roles in transforming the Christian mind and as a means of grace.[30] In a letter written in 1768 to Dr. Rutherforth, Wesley explains the role of cognitive thinking, or reason in the Methodist approach, noting, reason "is a fundamental principle with us, that to renounce reason is to renounce religion; that religion and reason go hand in hand; and that all irrational religion is false religion."[31] However, for Wesley, Scripture is for more than informing doctrine, it is intended as a transformative impetus of the human affections. Furthermore, it is the role of the Holy Spirit in Scripture that transforms the heart of an individual.

The Holy Spirit is described as an advocate on the behalf of Christians, and the Spirit of Truth (John 14:15–26). The Holy Spirit is the Third Person of the Trinity, equal to the Father and Son, representing completion in the divine life. The Spirit, or *ruach* in Hebrew, is described in feminine language. While in the Greek translation, the Holy Spirit is described as the *Paraklete*, or *Parakletos*, whom the Father and Son sent to be the constant companion

27. Rom 12:2.
28. Martin, *Jesuit Guide*, 119.
29. Martin, *Jesuit Guide*, 118.
30. Maddox, *Responsible Grace*, 40.
31. Wesley, "Letter to Dr. Rutherforth," 558.

of Christians. "Para" means in the presence of, before, and beside, while "Kleo" means to summon. In the book of Acts 2:2–13, the disciples and followers of Jesus gathered together at Pentecost and were baptized with the Holy Spirit and with "fire." This was in fulfillment of the prophecy from Joel 2:28: "And afterward, I will pour out my Spirit on all people. Your sons and daughters will prophesy, your old men will dream dreams, and your young men will see visions." This text is mentioned again in Acts 2:17: "In the last days, God says, I will pour out my Spirit on all people. Your sons and daughters will prophesy, your young men will see visions, your old men will dream dreams." The role of the Holy Spirit described in John 16:12–16 is to "guide you," or better, "will put you on the way" which is Christ, who notes, "I am the way" (John 14:6).

Wesley noted, "Let reason do all that reason can; employ it as far as it will go. But, at the same time, acknowledge it is utterly incapable of giving either faith, or hope, or love; and, consequently, of producing either real virtue, or substantial happiness. Expect these from a higher source, even from the Father of the spirits of all flesh."[32] Wesley captured the importance of experiencing both knowledge and heart felt love in spiritual formation. Wesley proclaimed,

> Unite the pair so long Disjoin'd,
> Knowledge and Vital Piety;
> Learning and Holiness combined,
> And truth and love, let all men see,
> In those who up to Thee we give,
> Thine, wholey thine, to die and live.[33]

Like Ignatian spirituality, Wesleyan cognitive thinking is deeply tied to the inward journey of the affections, heart, and life in the Spirit.

In such a highly technological society, millennials and recent generations have not known a time without the Internet, email, or cell phones. In an age of quick answers, it is easy to overlook

---

32. Wesley, "Sermon 70," 360.
33. Wesley, *Works*, 7:643–44.

the slow work of contemplation, spiritual discipline, and the inner work of the Holy Spirit. Engaging in the inner spiritual life requires the intentional and purposeful implementation of spiritual disciplines focused on the inward spiritual journey such as prayer and discernment, and an overarching attitude of reflection.

Jesuit theologian Burghardt explains contemplation and prayer as a "long, loving look at the real."[34] It is unhurried, awareness-building, pragmatic, and centered in love. Open to the slow work of discernment, prayer, and listening, Christians are encouraged to become aware of the active work of God in their daily lives. Álvarez expounds on this practical spiritual approach, noting, "Such experience demands an attitude of authenticity and rejects a stereotyped response. Our encounter with the mystery of God takes place in the midst of reality, not in some realm apart."[35] The daily practice of the Jesuit Examen prayer encourages an examination of conscious. The prayer begins with gratitude, an acknowledgement of sins, a review of God's presence in the day, asking God for forgiveness and asking for God's grace for the next day.[36] In the Jesuit approach to the interior life they remind individuals "to seek and find God in all things."[37]

Similar to the Jesuits, Wesley approached spiritual formation practically. Grounded in reality, Wesley described life with God as a continual journey of inspiration with the Holy Spirit. He explained the Christian's life with and response to the Spirit of God in the following way: "God's breathing into the soul, and the soul's breathing back what it first receives from God; a continual action of God upon the soul, and a re-action of the soul upon God; an unceasing presence of God, the loving, pardoning God, manifested to the heart, and perceived by faith; and an unceasing return of love, praise, and prayer, offering up all the thoughts of our hearts, all the words of our tongues, all the works of our hands, all our body, soul, and spirit, to be a holy sacrifice, acceptable unto God

---

34. Burghardt, "Contemplation," 89.
35. Álvarez, "Promotion of Justice," 12.
36. Martin, *Jesuit Guide*, 92.
37. Álvarez, "Promotion of Justice," 12.

in Christ Jesus."[38] For both Wesley and Ignatius, the practical, lived out expression of Gods love in service and care for others was an extension of a vital inner life with God.

From a lifestyle of reflection, self-awareness, prayer, and solitude, individuals can develop a greater understanding of the "other" and the desire to enter into community and an outward expression of faith. The interrelation between God and humanity can be traced to the very relational aspect of God: father, son and Holy Spirit.[39] From a space of relationship with God, and through the empowerment of the Holy Spirit, followers of Christ live out their faith in vital piety, or through outward acts of service.

For Wesley, knowledge and vital piety find expression through means of grace, including acts of service and justice on behalf of the poor and marginalized. Maddox notes, "Wesley correlates biblical language of the heart with our inmost soul, and then stresses how this inner orientation of a Christian properly manifests itself in outward branches like works of love and mercy. This would appear to make the heart the seat of the inner springs of our outward words and actions."[40] From a rich interior life with God, and led by the Holy Spirit, Wesleyan Christians were urged to live out their faith on behalf of humanity through care for the poor, the marginalized, and the forgotten.

In Catholic social teaching, there is an emphasis on pursuing the common good of all humanity, working toward solidarity, and a preferential option for the poor. Former Superior General of the Society of Jesus Fr. Pedro Arrupe asserted that social justice and an "other" focused life is essential to being both spiritual and human. He commented, "Only by being a man-or-woman-for-others does one become fully human, not only in the merely natural sense, but in the sense of being the 'spiritual' person of Saint Paul."[41] Arrupe recognized a need for solidarity with the marginalized, for loving the "other." He noted, "Today our prime educational objective

38. Wesley, "Sermon 19," 187.
39. Deut 6:4; John 10:30; 17:20–22; 1 John 5:7.
40. Maddox, "Change of Affections," 14.
41. Arrupe, "Men for Others," para. 65.

must be to form men-and-women-for-others; men and women who cannot even conceive of love of God which does not include love for the least of their neighbors."[42] Arrupe suggested that in our relationship with the world we must make sure that all are able to have a voice; this is an essential element of social justice and of the spiritual life.

---

42. Arrupe, "Men for Others," para. 2.

3

The Importance of Faith Conversations

FAITH CONVERSATIONS WITH PARENTS and adult figures, or as one student termed it, his "Jesus dads," played a significant role in the ease to which student participants developed their spiritual identity. Although each student in the individual interviews and focus groups indicated that faith was "fairly important," "important," or "extremely important" to her or his life, interestingly, the developmental influences on students' leadership and spiritual identity formation varied. The spiritual identity of student participants was formed from a combination of exposure to new ideas, transitionary periods, challenges, and the influence and mentoring of religious figures, parachurch mentors, peers, and particularly parental figures.

Student participants who grew up in households without a strong faith background struggled to figure out how to connect their faith with their identity. "Parents will generally observe the same religiosity in their offspring's lives as they do in their own. . . . And because children observe their parents closely, it should not surprise parents that their children know their hypocrisies—religious and otherwise."[1] Jan Amir commented, "No one in my family has a faith so I think that is what has influenced the separation of spirituality and faith."[2] Tristan Jones recalled, "I did come into faith . . . a bit later than some. . . . And so those [foundational values] . . . are still developing. . . . Now [my spiritual values] are definitely more intertwined."[3] The students who did not grow up in faith-based households sought religious and spiritual instruction mostly through mentoring from older adults and from peers in high school and college.

The participants, who grew up without regular or meaningful religious practices in his or her household, or no religious background, found the transition toward spiritual identity confusing and difficult. "Families are not the only teachers of popular American moral culture, but they are its first teachers and its primary facilitators. They either reinforce its inculcation through mainstream socializing agents, such as schools, churches, community organizations, and media."[4] Those with purposeful religious backgrounds and upbringings had mixed results in attaining a clear spiritual identity. How parents chose to approach the topic of spiritual and religious identity with their children made a significant impact in the acceptance and practice of religious and spiritual identity.

In most cases, when student participants specified little or no spiritual direction from parents, they indicated that in their spiritual journey, they were mentored and trained by older spiritual leaders such as youth leaders. Students also moved toward faith ownership through relationships with peers, and often following a period of struggle or exposure to new ideas. Living with and involved closely with parents for a majority of his or her life, a key influence in participants' spiritual identity formation remained parental influence.

1. Clydesdale, *First Year Out*, 62.
2. Amir, personal interview, November 4, 2016.
3. Jones, personal interview, November 11, 2016.
4. Clydesdale, *First Year Out*, 55.

Key Influencers in Spiritual Development

The role of family, particularly parents, strongly influenced the nurture and understanding of faith and religious values in the lives of student participants. Many of the students with strong Catholic faith identities came from strong Catholic family backgrounds, although some of the students struggled with family expectations and perceived pressure to adopt religious beliefs and practices.

Liam Black recalled the integration of faith and religion in his family upbringing: "My dad's oldest brother is actually a Catholic priest. So [in the] living room, my uncle had his handy dandy Eucharist that he brings along everywhere. [And] my mom is a Catholic third grade teacher."[5] Sara Green commented, "I have never known my life without it [Catholic faith]. Ever since I was born I was baptized. I come from a very Catholic family. My father has his masters in Catholicism."[6] Mass performed in the home is not a unique experience to Liam's Catholic upbringing. Coming from a conservative Catholic family Sara Green remarked, "We have had mass performed in our living room. . . . [Catholic faith] has just always been a huge part of my life. Every phase my family has ever gone through, our faith has always been a part of that."[7] Henri Brown likewise noted the integration of faith in his upbringing: "I guess the term cradle Catholic applies. . . . It was a super Catholic household. I had been exposed to other forms of Christianity of some sort . . . but I was . . . Catholic. I always knew that growing up."[8]

Faith was important in the family lives of many of the students that grew up in traditional Catholic homes. Katie Johnson asserted that growing up in a strongly traditional Catholic family the faith decisions of her siblings mattered to her parents, "My mom is very traditional Irish Catholic. And I'm the youngest of 8 kids so I have grown up with seeing how my siblings interact

---

5. Black, personal interview, November 4, 2016.
6. Green, personal interview, November 4, 2016.
7. Green, personal interview, November 4, 2016.
8. Brown, personal interview, November 10, 2016.

with their faith, which is ... not always in line with what my mom would like it to be."⁹

Growing up in a strongly conservative Catholic family, some of the students felt a tension between an expectation to keep their family religious tradition and personal faith ownership. Liam Black felt a tension to meet his parents' faith expectations: "[I] didn't know if I wanted to [be Catholic]. I more felt that I had to do it because at that point I was open to the religion, faith and spirituality. But I also felt like it was kind of expected of me to do that. Kind of like going to college it was expected of me."¹⁰ April Garcia noted that her parents' strong expectations to practice the Catholic faith influenced her early spiritual identity: "Growing up [I always] identified myself as spiritual but not actually knowing what that meant. Kind of like having that spirituality defined for me by my parents or this expectation that I had to go to church on Sunday or I had to go to youth group as a middle schooler just because my parents wanted me to study the Bible."¹¹ April experienced the monotony of going through the motions of the Catholic faith tradition without fully understanding or owning her beliefs: "I think I put it in my mind constantly that my parents want me to get confirmed so I will get confirmed. Or my parents want me to get my first communion so I will get my first communion because it is what they did and it is what their parents did."¹² At times April felt burdened by her mother's expectations: "It is what [my mom] grew up doing so it is kind of like her way or the highway. . . . I think I was suppressed of the opportunity to think about things from my own perspective."¹³

Sara Green, coming from a conservative Catholic family, acknowledged her upbringing as a low point in her faith: "I felt like I was being commanded to do all these things. We are going to pray the rosary as a family. I don't care if you want to do it. We are

9. Johnson, personal interview, November 4, 2016.
10. Black, personal interview, November 13, 2016.
11. Garcia, personal interview, November 12, 2016.
12. Garcia, personal interview, November 12, 2016.
13. Garcia, personal interview, November 12, 2016.

doing it as a family. I understood the good intentions behind all that and actions like that. But the verbal—I don't care if you want to do it, we are going to do it—just pushed me farther and farther away."[14] Students in strongly conservative Catholic households recognized a mixture of love and good intentions from parents, but also strong expectations and pressure to conform to spiritual ideology and beliefs.

Parental faith expectations, however, did not always have a negative impact on student faith development. Joy Smith noted, my mom "wanted me to be [Catholic]—that was pretty obvious." Yet, Joy maintained that she did not feel forced to choose the Catholic faith.[15] She commented on her upbringing, "We went to church every week. My grandparents were Catholic. It was never like a huge thing . . . we also were liberal Catholic."[16] She explained that her parents' own faith journey influenced their approach. Her parents came to faith late in life, and the decision to become Catholic was "intentional on their part and they wanted it to be the same for us—that we chose our church."[17] Joy Smith recalled, "Before we did confirmation, my mom gave us this book of the world religions. Had us read through all of that and ask questions before we chose to be confirmed in the Catholic Church. So, it was never forced. It was never like I felt like I had to be Catholic."[18]

Personal choice played a large role in whether students felt satisfied with their parental approach to spirituality. Lloyd White suggested that there is a difference between influence and pressure, noting, "My whole life [I] was told that my spirituality—not told but . . . influenced—to have spirituality that is based on the church and the sacraments."[19]

Oftentimes, parenting is described as a balance between warmth and control, or love and concern versus rules and

14. Green, personal interview, November 11, 2016.
15. Smith, personal interview, November 10, 2016.
16. Smith, personal interview, November 10, 2016.
17. Smith, personal interview, November 10, 2016.
18. Smith, personal interview, November 10, 2016.
19. White, personal interview, November 13, 2016.

The Importance of Faith Conversations

expectations for behavior for compliance. There are four common descriptions of parental styles: authoritative, authoritarian, permissive and disengaged.[20] Authoritative parents have high levels of compliance, requiring children to follow parental guidelines, and high levels of responsiveness, leading toward negotiation, compromise and conversation with their children. Adolescents with authoritative parents can show strong signs of independence, self-assurance, and high social skills.[21] Authoritarian parents, in contrast, have high expectations of rules and compliance, while giving little in terms of compassion and warmth. Permissive parents have fewer clear expectations for children's' behavior, but instead emphasize love and warmth. Disengaged parents have low response and low demand, requiring little of their children and giving little love or concern in return.

Parental approach to spiritual direction and instruction was often instrumental in how student leaders engaged with their faith, and their amount of internal struggle. During the transition of emerging adults to the college environment, parents are expected to provide an "infrastructure, a safety net, and general emotional support" while having a "relatively limited" role.[22] Although parents during college often are less involved, and although "teens may attend fewer religious services during the first year . . . at the year's end, they continue to affirm the religious identities that they formed within their family context."[23] The role of parents in explaining faith helped ease confusion for many students. Lloyd White found that the lack of spiritual direction from parents slowed down his ability to create a spiritual identity and to own his faith. He commented, "Spirituality was very confusing I think to me. Growing up in a Catholic home, but it wasn't really talked about. It was just kind of like you go to church on Sunday, awesome. But it was never a conversation. There wasn't anything more

---

20. Arnett and Hughes, *Adolescence and Emerging Adulthood*.
21. Collins and Lursen, "Parent-Adolescent Relationships."
22. Clydesdale, *First Year Out*, 207.
23. Clydesdale, *First Year Out*, 62–63.

than that."²⁴ Open and encouraging conversations with parents were instrumental for building a healthy spiritual and faith identity for many student participants.

Parents explaining their religious traditions and having conversations about faith encouraged students to explore new ideas of their faith identity. Lloyd White recalled, "We were driving in a really cool place one time. I think it was Lake Tahoe area.... [My dad] just looked over at me and was like ... by looking at this, I don't know how anyone could think there isn't somebody upstairs that made this. I was like, hmmmm. Everything is so intentionally designed and there are so many moving parts—that how could it just happen?"²⁵

After Liam Black told his mother that he didn't want to attend church, yet still believed in God, she challenged her son, explaining the importance of spending time with God: "Ok, if you don't go to church at all throughout the year, you have zero time with God. There are 52 weeks in a year. How many hours are in a week—I think it is 124. 124 times 52—she is like, 'All this time God has influenced you and you are not creating that relationship with him ... pretty selfish.' Kind of explained it in more terms that you could grab. That stuck with me."²⁶ Henri Brown noted the importance of spiritual conversations with his father. His dad explained his Catholic tradition and why they participated in the Catholic faith. He related, "As long as I can remember I have heard [the Catholic faith] articulate[d], not just reasons for belief but a personal story of, here is why I chose Catholicism. . . . I had it modeled in front of me."²⁷

Along with spiritual conversations, student participants were encouraged by the role modeling of faith from their parents. Henri Brown explained his spiritual engagement with his father, "If I was a little kid I would tell my dad—is that really Catholic? He would go no, you're right and he would change his answer right in front of

24. White, personal interview, November 13, 2016.
25. White, personal interview, November 13, 2016.
26. Black, personal interview, November 13, 2016.
27. Brown, personal interview, November 10, 2016.

The Importance of Faith Conversations

me."[28] Henri explained the influence and impression that his father left on his life: "The way that you hear me talk [about faith] is a way that I heard my dad talk literally as long as I could remember."[29] For students such as Henri and Liam, their parents strongly influenced the understanding of faith integration. Observing his own parents' relationship, Liam desired to date and marry a Roman Catholic woman who shared similar beliefs and values. He spoke about his parents: "What makes them successful in marriage? It always came down to just faith and spirituality. No matter how bad it got . . . you could pray together or you could pray for the other person and the other person would pray for you."[30] Role modeling, and conversations about faith with parents in an open and engaging manner helped to develop faith and spiritual identity among student participants, yet strongly held parental expectations were often detrimental to student participants' ownership and development.

When forced to participate in faith practices with little say, students internally resisted. Traditional parenting styles, as first described by Baumrind,[31] requires a high level of responsiveness from the child, not encouraging discussion and debate, but instead, compliance by supporting the authority of the parent. Sara Green noted her resistance to her father's traditional parenting approach: "I hated the church, I hated going to mass, and I hated anything related to it, not because I personally didn't like God. But I didn't like how my father was facilitating that and ingraining that in my brothers and I."[32]

Parental conflict tends to increase during adolescence, with frequent conflict between mothers and daughters[33] and only declines in late adolescence and into emerging adulthood.[34] While in

---

28. Brown, personal interview, November 10, 2016.
29. Brown, personal interview, November 10, 2016.
30. Black, personal interview, November 13, 2016.
31. Baumrind, "Developmental Perspective on Adolescent Risk."
32. Green, personal interview, November 11, 2016.
33. Collins and Laursen, "Parent-Adolescent Relationships."
34. Cui et al., "Young Adult Romantic Relationships"; Dworkin and Larson, "Age Trends"; Gordon, "A(p)parent Play."

Unscripted Spirituality

High School Liam Black related the conflict between himself and his parents regarding his spirituality and faith as he transitioned from high school to college, "I was feeling the pressure from [my parents] to put in more effort. And feeling the pressure from what I felt my parents were putting on me to go more religiously. I was just like . . . what If I don't want to do this? And kind of realizing ok, if I don't want to I can—not do that. That is kind of what led to more [spiritual] highs."[35]

Although Liam felt strongly pressured toward choosing the Catholic faith, students like April and Liam argued in retrospect that their parents did not intend to force them or put such heavy expectations on them. Clydesdale explained that although parental relationships "fade[d] into the background" during college, and grew "a little awkward" they also became "more valued."[36] April Garcia explained, "I have always grown up being really hard on myself because I really like to live up to people's expectations. I think I put it in my mind constantly that my parents want me to get confirmed so I will get confirmed. Or my parents want me to get my first communion so I will get my first communion because it is what they did and it is what their parents did."[37] The more room parents allowed their children, the quicker their children found freedom in developing spiritual identity and faith ownership. Joy Smith explained, "I didn't feel as though I have to [become Catholic] for my mom or anything like that. I think because of that, coming [to GU], I knew I had made that commitment to myself and I wanted to still have that part of myself."[38]

In raising spiritually aware children, parents have to find a tricky balance of influencing and dictating their child's decisions and practices. The freedom to choose a faith practice released students from internal pressure to please their parents, while students with little to no faith conversations with parents internalized confusion and a strong desire for spiritual clarity.

    35. Black, personal interview, November 13, 2016.
    36. Clydesdale, *First Year Out*, 93.
    37. Garcia, personal interview, November 12, 2016.
    38. Smith, personal interview, November 10, 2016.

Mentoring Communities in Faith Conversations

Along with parents, mentors and peers also played a large role in the developmental influences and formation of the spiritual identity of student participants. Peer mentors, even a year or two older were influential. Parks recommends a mentoring community to help emerging adults develop a complex faith life. She explains, [A mentoring community] "offers a network of belonging in which young adults feel recognized as who they really are, and as who they are becoming. It offers both challenges and support and thus offers good company for both the emerging strength and the distinctive vulnerability of the young adult."[39] April Garcia noted the significance of her retreat student leader in helping her move toward faith ownership: "I had the small group leader and she was the first person to question me on why I practiced that faith."[40] Depth of conversation and freedom to explore new ideas opened up new opportunities for faith formation.

Liam Black noted the importance of developing relationships with friends who shared his faith background. Although he had not had many Catholic friends in High School, he felt that faith "develops who you are in a different way. If you are friends with people who aren't religious based, then you are likely to not be as religious yourself."[41] This led Liam to desire "some good friends who are religious" and to be "in a relationship [with a woman] who was religious and Catholic specifically."[42]

Even as early as high school, Lloyd White maintained that his friends in high school helped to explain new concepts in faith; they "really taught me that the walls [could] totally be broken down. It is not this cookie cutter faith thing that a lot of people have."[43] Without consistent conversations about faith at home,

---

39. Parks, *Big Questions, Worthy Dreams*, 95.
40. Garcia, personal interview, November 12, 2016.
41. Black, personal interview, November 13, 2016.
42. Black, personal interview, November 13, 2016.
43. White, personal interview, November 13, 2016.

Unscripted Spirituality

Lloyd observed the continued importance of peers in college to challenge and raise new ideas in faith.[44] When approaching times of brokenness, Lloyd White reasserted that during college his friends who shared his faith beliefs had become his "full time support system."[45] In forming his spiritual identity, Lloyd found connecting with peers spiritually to be essential to his personal faith development: "I think depth of conversation is a huge piece of, to wrestle with those big topics."[46] Lloyd explained the significance: "I think having people my age who were willing to be vulnerable and actually wrestle with the questions that I had and go through that spiritual journey with me played a huge role. . . . To have people that would day in, day out, walk alongside me . . . and dig a little deeper."[47]

Shared faith and values with friends helped support Lloyd in times of suffering and confusion as well. He reiterated, "Having a place where you can go home at the end of a really crappy day and literally cry if you want and have people that will listen and sit with you. Not talk at you but be with you in that space is super, super awesome."[48]

April Garcia explained that her friends help her to be authentic, helping her to address spiritual darkness in her life. She recalled, "I had three good friends in particular come up to me and say, hey you know we have noticed you have been a little off. Or maybe just haven't had the same energy or the same excitement for things—where is this coming from?"[49] However, peers did not always bring students closer to exploring their faith, but at times had negative impacts. Joy Smith noted that when she initially began college, she was not spending time with people who shared the same values. She asserted, "That negatively impacted me. But it also positively impacted me because it forced me to realize there

44. White, personal interview, November 13, 2016.
45. White, personal interview, November 13, 2016.
46. White, personal interview, November 13, 2016.
47. White, personal interview, November 13, 2016.
48. White, personal interview, November 13, 2016.
49. Garcia, personal interview, November 12, 2016.

The Importance of Faith Conversations

was a disconnect in the way I was acting and the way I wanted and knew I was."[50]

Local parishes and churches have also played a role in influencing student leaders, particularly during high school and college. Megan Pile noted that although "self-conscience of not growing up with religion," she felt welcomed into the church.[51] She found that, in "a lot of ways, I have been given a lot of my faith."[52] At the age of eight or nine years old, Liam Black began exploring his faith during a reconciliation class put on by his church. Looking back, Liam assessed that although he hated his class, "At the same time I could understand what the significance of what we were doing as a faith—I didn't know how that played to me and to the community, [what] the value of that was. But it helped me understand more the relationship with God—deepen that or start cultivating that a little bit more."[53] Students managed to find their own faith voice, some being mentored in faith by non-family members, such as youth group and parachurch ministry leaders, or by attending faith based schools.

Parachurch organizations like Young Life also played a role in helping to shape some students' spiritual practices and theology. Tristan Jones recalled that while at a Young Life event, "I really connected with God and Jesus as like the center [of my life] . . . this relationship with Jesus. That was really put into perspective personally, kind of bringing religion into my personal life and faith into my personal life. And not just on Wednesday nights or at [church] on Sundays."[54] Parish priests, youth leaders, along with Christian camp staff, spiritually directed students, shared theology and assisted during crisis. Priests at Gonzaga and University Ministry staff also helped to provide direction and clarity in times of distress and spiritual crisis.

---

50. Smith, personal interview, November 10, 2016.
51. Pile, focus group interview, November 3, 2016.
52. Pile, focus group interview, November 3, 2016.
53. Black, personal interview, November 13, 2016.
54. Jones, personal interview, November 11, 2016.

Unscripted Spirituality

Tristan Jones, growing up without a strong faith identity in his home, noted the relational aspect of his faith, and the importance of "people and community," which has "been a really big part of my spirituality."[55] He admitted the importance of two faith mentors he met through a parachurch ministry in high school, calling them his "Jesus dads."[56]

Leaders at a Christian camp likewise revealed new ways of exploring faith for Tristan Jones. He noted, "They were such joyful people . . . you could see that difference and they pointed to Jesus."[57] Tristan Jones eventually connected to another mentor in college that he met through a parachurch group, explaining the care and kindness he was shown, "He just pours into people. He will send birthday gifts and books and things and be like let's all read this book, I heard it is really cool. . . . We have been having this morning text devotional going for like . . . over a year and a half."[58]

This mentor not only texted devotionals each morning, helped run a men's small group in the summer, but also continues to speak "positivity into our life—like you can do this, God is putting things on your hearts. Listen to it, lean into it sort of thing. He has just been a really loving voice in my life."[59] Not coming from a faith upbringing, Tristan saw his mentors as "role models on how to live out faith . . . bringing Christ more into [my] life and just building that relationship and being more intentional with [my] time and faith."[60] Mentors in close relationship with students had the ability to speak into difficult times, explaining suffering, and the role of God in our lives. Tristan Jones' mentor explained faith and theology adeptly, noting, "God is not a feeling. Sure, joy and

---

55. Jones, focus group interview, November 3, 2016.
56. Jones, personal interview, November 11, 2016.
57. Jones, personal interview, November 11, 2016.
58. Jones, personal interview, November 11, 2016.
59. Jones, personal interview, November 11, 2016.
60. Jones, personal interview, November 11, 2016.

peace are ways he works. But faith in itself is kind of doing and trusting in God."[61]

Jessie Gray recalled her middle school and high school youth director as a "loved and trusted" mentor.[62] She commented that she and her former director still have a daily "streak going of snap chats."[63] Jessie acknowledged, "She is just really a rock for me in my faith because a lot of other people that I'm close to are very wavering . . . whether it is my friends, my family. So she was definitely someone that I talked to a lot."[64]

April Garcia also expressed the importance of her high school youth leader, as a guide to better understanding and owning her faith. She noted,

> She was just the most amazing woman and just really pushed us out of our comfort zone with doing service work and going to church. . . . She was the first person I think to help me see that spirituality isn't seeing so much in a Bible or in a scripture reading or in the word that the priest is saying. It is more like what you see in your interactions with people. She did that by helping us get on the streets and work with the homeless or encouraging us on the weekends to come and help volunteer within the church and interact with people.[65]

However, experiences with churches and church leaders were not all positive for student participants. Jessie Gray recalled a particularly trying experience in her bible study when she was told her sister, who had become an atheist, was not spiritually secure: "I had a Bible study leader basically tell me that my sister was going to go to hell. I was like ok. I'm a junior in high school. I'm not prepared to handle a conversation like this. . . . She wasn't trying

---

61. Jones, personal interview, November 11, 2016.
62. Gray, personal interview, November 12, 2016.
63. Gray, personal interview, November 12, 2016.
64. Gray, personal interview, November 12, 2016.
65. Garcia, personal interview, November 12, 2016.

to be hurtful. I think that she was trying to encourage me and call me to action . . . [but] that was not an effective approach for me."[66]

Liam Black also had a difficultly coming against the conservative and traditional teachings of church leaders at his parish. He remembered his deacon noting, "We are telling you what to do, this is how we do it and you need to follow it. I dug my heels in, kicking and screaming the whole way. . . . I was like nope. Not having this."[67] The spiritual influence of the church, family members and peers can have both negative and positive influences upon a student.

---

66. Gray, personal interview, November 12, 2016.
67. Black, personal interview, November 13, 2016.

4

The Development of Spiritual Identity

During college students are often faced with life's big questions. Liam Black recalled such a time: "I could never determine without a higher deity or some type of faith—Why are we here? Are we just here to exist to get the best life as possible?"[1] College can be a significant time of differentiation from family and societal belief systems and a discovery of new ways of thinking and being. The exploration of identity and faith ownership can often occur during times of transition and change, such as being immersed into a new college environment. Often away from family and networks of belonging, students are faced with questions of identity: "Who am I?" "What do I believe?" "What really matters to me?" Student participants recalled the exploration of their faith identity when exposed to new ways of thinking and practice, during periods of suffering, and through spiritual encounters with the holy.

The journey toward spiritual identity takes time, and is often unsettling, leaving some students like Jan Amir uncertain of their faith identity. Jan Amir explained, "I don't know if I necessarily

---

1. Black, personal interview, November 13, 2016.

connect my faith with my spirituality just because I don't even know how to define my faith right now. . . . No one in my family has a faith so I think that is what has influenced the separation of spirituality and faith. Sometimes I don't even feel comfortable talking about God or talking about my faith because I'm still growing a lot and still don't know a lot."[2] Those students that had engaged in open and exploratory faith conversations with family, mentors, and peers prior to college felt more prepared and less anxious in determining what they believed. Some student participants, such as Sara Green faced her spiritual identity as a battleground.

Sara Green explained that her identity is difficult to process with the felt tension between her belief systems, her family, and politics, noting, "With my family . . . it is like [they] make it seem impossible to be a liberal and a Catholic at the same time. I'm battling all these different beliefs and values."[3] Figuring out more liberal beliefs about abortion or gay marriage puts her faith in a place of tension. Sara Green explained her understanding of spirituality and faith as a separation of Catholic belief and values and her spiritual "friendship with God."[4] She continued her identity exploration, "Well then what does it mean to be Catholic? Does that mean I have to believe this, does that mean I have to believe that—does it not matter? Whether or not I think this is right or wrong does that mean I am any less Catholic? So, I think I'm currently on the journey of figuring that out."[5] Sara concluded, "Maybe I'm not at a time in my life where I can call myself Catholic because I don't want to dishonor whatever that may be if I'm in this limbo. But I am spiritual with God."[6]

For some young adults, organized religion, along with modern thought, is considered restricting and intolerant of others' opinions and ideas. Possibly for this reason, young adults in the postmodern world appear to be moving away from organized

2. Amir, focus group interview, November 4, 2016.
3. Green, personal interview, November 11, 2016.
4. Green, personal interview, November 11, 2016.
5. Green, personal interview, November 11, 2016.
6. Green, personal interview, November 11, 2016.

religion. According to the Gallup polls, instead of identifying with organized religion, educated emerging adults in the United States between the ages of eighteen and twenty-nine are self-identifying in the category of no religious affiliation, or "none." "The rise in *nones* partly reflects changes in the general pattern of expression of religion in American society today—particularly including trends towards more *unbranded*, casual, informal religion."[7] Educators could interpret informal belief as an indication that students have no desire for religious guidance or spiritual support. As organized religion moves from the center of postmodern American life to the edges, the less formal inclination does not indicate that today's emerging adults are less spiritually inclined.

The spiritual experience of emerging adults looks different than prior generations, indicating openness, and less structure. Cherry, DeBerg, and Porterfield conducted research among four different types of schools around the United States to determine students' religious experiences. The authors found that most students expressed a strong sense of pluralism, they were "spiritual seekers rather than religious dwellers, and many of them were constructing their spirituality without much regard to the boundaries dividing religious denominations, traditions or organizations."[8] Postmodernism has affected the religious lives of emerging adults, moving from rigidity toward a less structured and evolving faith life. In a study conducted with the Templeton foundation in 2002, Chickering and coauthors noted that students are no longer following in the steps of their grandparents or parents. They are not constrained to denominations, or even necessarily particular religious ideals, but their beliefs and values are fluid and anamorphous.[9]

Many of the student participants in this study asserted that their faith and spirituality was important to them and extremely important to them had strong spiritual identities. Jessie Gray maintained, "Faith and spirituality is such a big part of my identity

---

7. Saad, "Rise in Religious 'Nones,'" para. 4.
8. Cherry et al., *Religion on Campus*, 276–77.
9. Chickering et al., *Encouraging Authenticity*.

and who I am."[10] Growing up in the Catholic Church, Sara Green explained how her Catholic faith and spirituality is intertwined with her very self-identity, "I have never known my life without [my spiritual identity]. Even though sometimes my faith is the most frustrating thing in my life, it is still what I cling to at the end of the day just because it has been the most consistent thing in my life."[11] In forming her spiritual and faith identity, Joy Smith conceded her decision to continue in her Catholic faith is tied to her personal values: "I really loved that part of my identity because . . . I really think that the core of the Catholic Church—the core of the dignity of all human beings—is so firmly rooted in my values. I love the identity of being Catholic."[12] Yet the spiritual faith journey is not easily attained for many student participants, as it involves questioning, suffering, and exposure to new ideas and beliefs. During unsettling periods of transition, by being exposed to new ideas, and through spiritual encounters with the holy, students are faced with making a decision toward a spiritual identity and path.

The Role of Transitions in Spiritual Growth

Faith ownership became an important milestone for students during high school and particularly when they attended college. Periods of transition are important in the development of identity and in feeling secure in self and place. Fowler noted the spiritual transitions of children (ages 7–12) from the mythic stage, where faith is understood in literal terms, toward a conventional faith (ages 12 to adult), where individuals might build a spiritual and personal identity.[13] Individuals might remain in a stage without further progressing. In the conventional faith stage, where many emerging adults are forming their spiritual identities, they may decide to stay with a recognized belief system and avoid uncertainty.

10. Gray, focus group interview, November 4, 2016.
11. Green, focus group interview, November 4, 2016.
12. Smith, focus group interview, November 3, 2016.
13. Fowler, *Stages of Faith*.

To transition to the fourth stage, emerging adults must experience turmoil, making decisive decisions to make sense of the conflicts and tensions of their spirituality and lived out experiences.

For college students, major transitions and exposure to new belief systems can lead toward growth and spiritual development. For example, the transition for college students in a residential college takes them from a comfortable and known home environment, toward an uncertain and often confusing space. In this new space, students are often faced with making life decisions relating to their faith and practices. Joy Smith observed that many of her Catholic friends who transitioned to college struggled to make faith their own: "They are proud to say they are Catholic and they still go to mass when they go home but [their faith] kind of fades away. I think that is because . . . they haven't taken the time to make it their own."[14] Upon transitioning to college, Megan Pile began to ask herself, "Is this [faith] mine or is this someone else's?"[15] She recalled that in her first year she attended a student-led worship group and "found God."[16] She explained, "There was this moment where I felt, oh my God, I think I believe in God. It was really cool."[17] Megan noted, "I came to Gonzaga without a faith and have slowly, quickly in some ways, been given one."[18] Student participants related that when they decided to own their faith and spirituality, they were experiencing times of transition, either in attending college for the first time, attending a faith based school in high school, or by exposure to new ideas.

Joy Smith found that once she started attending college, "I started going to student mass and it was my own. Even when I was . . . really low, the mass was something that I loved. I realized this was something I get to grow through" a way to "build up my own personal faith."[19] Transitioning to college and connecting

14. Smith, personal interview, November 10, 2016.
15. Pile, focus group interview, November 3, 2016.
16. Pile, focus group interview, November 3, 2016.
17. Pile, focus group interview, November 3, 2016.
18. Pile, focus group interview, November 3, 2016.
19. Smith, personal interview, November 10, 2016.

with like-minded students was difficult for Joy. She commented, "If I said can I go to church with you guys—for some reason that felt like such a hurdle for me. I think that is because I was in this place where they all think I'm this person that I'm not. But also, I think I learned . . . it is not so black and white because I wasn't being myself but I was being myself."[20] Many of her friends did not attend mass with her, yet, Joy Smith stated, "even though they weren't friends through my faith journey, they were friends in the sense that I needed to go through that maybe and realize that I can do faith on my own. That is where I started making this realization that it is how I can get stronger in [my faith]. . . . It really became my own."[21] In college Joy Smith felt that making friends with similar faith values was a way for her to embrace her spiritual identity. She explains, "Even by doing that . . . made me feel like I was owning my faith."[22]

April Garcia was challenged by her roommate her first month in college to reassess her faith and practices. Exposed to new ideas and beliefs by her roommate, April recalled,

> My roommate wasn't religious. She would constantly question me like, "It is ok if you miss Mass tonight. You don't have to go, you are really stressed out." I would be like, "No; I have to go to mass. I have never missed mass." She was like, "Well what are you going to get out of that hour? Would you be more productive if you are doing homework?" She would constantly question me on those things. I remember one night skipping Mass and thinking—let's see how productive I am. I was productive and that was the first time I was thinking, why do I go to mass?[23]

April explained that in forming her spiritual identity in college, she opted to practice her Catholic faith in new ways, "Mass isn't something that I feel like there is so much expected of me

20. Smith, personal interview, November 10, 2016.
21. Smith, personal interview, November 10, 2016.
22. Smith, personal interview, November 10, 2016.
23. Garcia, personal interview, November 12, 2016.

anymore. I feel like it is just something that I kind of am able to take at my own pace. Cause no one is there watching me, expecting me to do the motions."[24]

April clarified that in college she has been able to redefine her Catholic faith so that she can live it authentically. While abroad, April also was exposed to new spiritual ideas and practices. She mentioned, "[There] was so much spirituality in the people I would interact with. These conversations where they had so much depth and they had so much insight. Being able to relate to somebody who has a totally different lifestyle from me and grew up in a totally different family setting and has different beliefs than me and can hardly even speak my language. But being able to break down those barriers through things like . . . laughter or through just sitting and being with people."[25] April's definition of spirituality grew during her time abroad. She asserted that she experienced more spirituality through "being uncomfortable and being in a new setting, than I have ever seen in a church setting."[26] She explained that although there were religious and nonreligious students, and students practicing different faith traditions, "All of us would be able to get something really deep and meaningful out of the interactions and the activities we do in the environment there, but it meant something different for everyone. That was the first time I saw just the vastness of spirituality and how diverse spirituality can be."[27]

For April, faith is: "Something that you can see in yourself and that you manifest in yourself. It doesn't have to be from going to Mass every Sunday."[28] Instead, April noted that her spiritual practices can include "getting engaged with [University Ministry] and getting engaged with the people who really want to share that faith with me."[29] In developing faith ownership, students noted

24. Garcia, personal interview, November 12, 2016.
25. Garcia, personal interview, November 12, 2016.
26. Garcia, personal interview, November 12, 2016.
27. Garcia, personal interview, November 12, 2016.
28. Garcia, personal interview, November 12, 2016.
29. Garcia, personal interview, November 12, 2016.

their personal approaches to faith, and how they made sense of their experiences. Interestingly, for many Catholic participants, faith ownership also included exposure to different types of thinking and spiritual practices, such as the Protestant Evangelical tradition.

Exposure to New Belief Systems

Many of the Catholic and Protestant student leaders recalled periods when their religious identity was challenged by their exposure to new faith practices. On first year student retreat, April Garcia indicated that at Gonzaga, "everyone is so open to an open dialogue about whatever you believe in."[30] She found the open faith environment to be positive and uplifting, compared to her more narrowly defined Catholic upbringing. She explained, "Everyone pushes you to believe in whatever spirituality you want to believe in, whether that is religious based or not. That was something that I really loved about it. I loved that I could have conversations with my really good friends who were Protestant. I could have really good conversations with the girl down the hall who is Atheist. We all kind of share in this open dialogue about spirituality."[31] The environment at Gonzaga encouraged some of the students to engage deeper in their faith, and feel affirmed, while some students found the openness to all religious backgrounds difficult for their affirmation of faith and spiritual identity.

Once exposed to new faith traditions, each student participant responded in different ways, some clinging to their identity as Catholic, while others found the faith practices and theology of other religious traditions, such as the Protestant faith, more compelling to their personal spiritual identity. In their longitudinal study of college students and spiritual development, Holcomb and Nonneman identified three types of crisis most frequently experienced by college students with greater faith growth and

30. Garcia, personal interview, November 12, 2016.
31. Garcia, personal interview, November 12, 2016.

The Development of Spiritual Identity

development: exposure to diverse thinking, multicultural exposure, and general life and emotional challenges.[32] For some of the student participants, when they were exposed to new faith beliefs and practices, they transitioned from nominal Catholic or nonreligious households to the Protestant faith.

A key to owning faith and spiritual identity involves periods of transition, whether through being exposed to new belief systems, such as Evangelical traditions for Catholic students, or transitioning to college, or being challenged in meaningful faith conversations with friends who are atheists. Lloyd White described his faith ownership and identity formation as a "journey of spirituality and faith" and a "process of going through ups and downs," like a "monitor in a hospital."[33] In the following section, I will share the faith journeys and periods of transition of Tristan Jones, Lloyd White, Liam Black, April Garcia, and Henri Brown.

Tristan Jones grew up within a non-Christian household with strong relational values. He noted that when he first began to attend church, after an invitation from friends, he viewed church and church activities initially as "fun" and non-committal, a minor background to his life.[34] He began attending youth group to be with childhood friends, yet during sophomore in high school, "words definitely started taking more meaning and just having more weight in my heart."[35] He recalled his conversion experience as a moment in time when he chose to become a follower of Christ: "I went on my first missions trip that next summer. Gave my life to Christ there. That was a really powerful moment. I feel like that was—I mean you know that is the beginning of your faith life. I remember flying back on the airplane home and feeling like I had a new set of eyes."[36] Yet somehow, not growing up within a family with a strong religious background, Tristan Jones felt he needed to "catch up" in faith, not knowing "any scripture" or "any

32. Holcomb and Nonneman, "Faithful Change," 101.
33. White, focus group interview, November 3, 2016.
34. Jones, personal interview, November 11, 2016.
35. Jones, personal interview, November 11, 2016.
36. Jones, personal interview, November 11, 2016.

of these songs that they are closing their eyes and singing to."[37] Tristan Jones recalled the times of prayer in his household: "My dad grew up in the Catholic Church and was you know, 'Come Lord Jesus,' I guess. 'Amen' sort of thing. [Prayer] was [for] our house, our family, our health, and if someone was traveling, it was like 'be with them.' It was so—through the motions. We didn't have a big, personal faith life within my household."[38]

Lloyd White grew up in a Catholic home, yet found his faith in junior high and high school while attending a Protestant school. He recalled his time there: "[Faith] is a part of everything we do. It is relationships, it is everything, it is huge. It plays a role in every single step we take. Very different, very confusing. I remember so we would have chapel every Wednesday. I remember the first one I walked into and I was like what the heck is this. Where is the priest? It was so foreign to me, I didn't know there was something else out there."[39] Lloyd tried to figure out more about the Protestant and Catholic perspectives: "Do they believe in the same thing or are there differences. Why do some people that are on both sides not get along?"[40]

While in high school Lloyd White recalled "going through that preliminary process of trying to figure [faith] out. Now that I feel like I have it a little bit more figured out, I'm more comfortable [and can] remain true to that—more authentic to that."[41] When interacting with students in college who "didn't see the world the same as I do," Lloyd White felt his strong faith identity, initially formed in high school "allowed me to be comfortable with myself enough to have those in depth conversations and authentic conversations that I really do enjoy having."[42] When Lloyd told his Italian, Catholic family he wanted to attend a Protestant church, he recalled his family's initial response: "You want to go to a different

37. Jones, personal interview, November 11, 2016.
38. Jones, personal interview, November 11, 2016.
39. White, personal interview, November 13, 2016.
40. White, personal interview, November 13, 2016.
41. White, personal interview, November 13, 2016.
42. White, personal interview, November 13, 2016.

kind of church? What? I got a lot of pushback on that for a while."[43] Yet after deciding to practice a Protestant faith, he recalled his parents' response: "I think once my parents and family [felt] like, ok this kid is old enough—this is something he has to figure out for himself. And . . . I think coming to Gonzaga there are a lot of people in the same boat. . . . Even walking up and down the aisle at Branches, [a Protestant nondenominational church], you see people who may have come from Catholic backgrounds."[44]

He noted, "I have kind of joked for the longest time saying that I'm kind of the mix of the best of both worlds . . . I have kind of pulled from both. But I would definitely fall on the Protestant side."[45] Liam Black, coming from a strong Catholic family background, found that in high school, following periods of difficulty, he began observing the differences between people with and without a faith identity, "I could see the distinct dynamic of people who had religion and who didn't . . . and how that played an impact on the way they carried themselves. In the classroom, on the sports field or court, and how they just treated people."[46]

Through exposure to people with Baptist and Protestant faith practices and beliefs in high school, Liam Black began exploring his spiritual identity; "I ended up spending a lot of time with them and kind of talking about faith."[47] One of the formative turning points for Liam was his family's decision to allow him space to choose his own faith practices; "I didn't go to church every Sunday because we had to. . . . That kind of started . . . [me] seeing [faith] from a new light."[48]

April Garcia recognized that upon arriving at Gonzaga her first year of college she had to figure out her own Catholic spiritual identity, "For the first time [I was] able to advocate for my faith. I think that my freshmen year was the first time . . . I was like, 'Why

43. White, personal interview, November 13, 2016.
44. White, personal interview, November 13, 2016.
45. White, personal interview, November 13, 2016.
46. Black, personal interview, November 13, 2016.
47. Black, personal interview, November 13, 2016.
48. Black, personal interview, November 13, 2016.

am I Catholic?' I had never actually asked why? Or do I actually want to believe in this? Now it is my choice. No one else can make this choice for me, it is actually my choice."[49] Although April Garcia feels her faith is "definitely something I'm still figuring out," she notes her time at Gonzaga is "the first time I [am] really excited to be Catholic."[50]

April Garcia reiterated, "Since coming to college, it is the first time I have been able to look at my religion in comparison to other religions. I find so much beauty in so many branches of Christianity."[51] Through ecumenical conversations with peers in college, and exposure to new beliefs and practices, April asserted, "I don't think I saw that beauty [in faith] until I was able to see what everyone was experiencing."[52] While attending Protestant services, April said, "I always just feel like there is . . . this missing thing. . . . I really think it is just the Eucharist."[53]

Henri Brown, raised in a strongly practicing Catholic household, recalled the tension he felt in defining his spiritual identity while attending an Evangelical high school: "I was exposed to this world of Evangelical theology for so long and the belief system. For a while I thought about going with it."[54] At home, Henri Brown recalled that his family would often say, "We are Catholic and we are going to stay Catholic." Henri reflected on that time, noting although he was not "buying what they are selling, . . . that was interesting to be in that environment for so long and to really kind of have no choice but to academically learn about it. Not only to learn about it but to learn about it inside out and to be able to explain it and defend it in a way when you don't want to."[55]

However, Henri notes that although he does not consider himself Evangelical, he was influenced by their approach to

---

49. Garcia, personal interview, November 12, 2016.
50. Garcia, personal interview, November 12, 2016.
51. Garcia, personal interview, November 12, 2016.
52. Garcia, personal interview, November 12, 2016.
53. Garcia, personal interview, November 12, 2016.
54. Brown, personal interview, November 10, 2016.
55. Brown, personal interview, November 10, 2016.

The Development of Spiritual Identity

spirituality and theology. "I jokingly now call myself an evangelized Catholic. Just because some of the ways I now understand Catholicism."[56] Henri Brown declared, in a typically Evangelical way, "You have to be willing to push the envelope in terms of saying this is who I am, this is what I believe and I'm not willing to compromise on that."[57] In being exposed to new beliefs and new faith practices, Henri Brown and his peers were able to find greater clarity in discerning their spiritual identities.

The Importance of Spiritual Experience

Key to clarifying spiritual identity, were moments when students encountered the Holy Spirit, the presence of the living Christ. Spiritual experience plays a significant role in opening an individual's heart to what has only been previously cognitively realized. According to Wenger, in education, "an excessive emphasis on formalism without corresponding levels of participation ... can easily result in an experience of meaninglessness."[58] Similarly, in spiritual identity formation, without spiritual experience the spiritual life can seem solely an intellectual endeavor, and ultimately, meaningless, while spiritual participation with God can create a deeper sense of self, ownership and identity.

The student participants expressed multiple moments of spiritual connection with God and the Holy Spirit as influential toward faith ownership. While leading the worship group on campus, Tristan saw the experience as "a really cool way of seeing the patience and handy work of God all connected."[59] In reflection, Tristan saw the way God led each individual to be involved, and "how those people bring their own stories and energy to the group."[60] The spiritual experience opened Tristan's eyes to the work

---

56. Brown, personal interview, November 10, 2016.
57. Brown, personal interview, November 10, 2016.
58. Wenger, *Communities of Practice*, 67.
59. Jones, focus group interview, November 3, 2016.
60. Jones, focus group interview, November 3, 2016.

of God in his life, and in the lives of all those students involved in the worship group.

Álvarez explains that the Ignatian principle of the "experience of the real" creates an awareness of truth and reality. He expounds on this idea, "Such experience demands an attitude of authenticity and rejects a stereotyped response. Our encounter with the mystery of God takes place in the midst of reality, not in some realm apart."[61] In other words, "we are called to seek and find God in all things."[62] Spiritual experiences often happen during periods of challenge, while students are often in transition. Students explained the many ways that God was present during their periods of transition, and the ways they attempted to seek him.

Joy Smith noted that she felt most connected with God during one of the lowest periods of her life; this time was while living abroad and struggling with a personal life crisis. She recalled visiting a church in Europe, "I walked around and saw all the ornate decorations and I got to one and realized they are about adoration. So I sat down and I just pulled out my journal and started journaling. I started adoration and sat there for a minute and kept journaling . . . it is kind of like a prayer. . . . I looked up at the Eucharist and looked down at my journal and something clicked in my head that I was literally talking to God. . . . I walked out of that church and I felt the most connected to God I think I have ever felt in my entire life."

During a stressful time during her final year of high school, Sara Green recalled a time when she visited the famous Our Lady of Lourdes statue from Lourdes, France, that was being shown at her local church. Sara explained her experience, "I drove to the church and it was dark, there were two other people in there. I went and just knelt in front of her and there was this beautiful light illuminating her. She just looked beautiful. All my life, statues have just been statues, but I looked at her and a bunch of emotions just came pouring out. I just started crying."[63] Sara continued,

61. Álvarez, "Promotion of Justice," 12.
62. Álvarez, "Promotion of Justice," 12.
63. Green, personal interview, November 11, 2016.

The Development of Spiritual Identity

> I had this profound experience of wow, you really love me. You really love me. No matter what I do, no matter what I say, no matter how I may push God away or you away. You are just going to love me and it felt—this is going to sound so crazy—but it felt like she was an actual living being. She didn't look porcelain. She didn't look like a statue. She looked like a physical being. It was a very profound [moment]. I was bawling like I can't believe this love is consuming and engulfing me right now.[64]

Spiritual experiences can often be profound, affecting an individual emotionally, spiritually and mentally.

In deciding which college to attend, Sara Green felt torn between Gonzaga and Loyola Chicago. Her dad suggested praying to God and looking at the tabernacle in her local church. "He's like sweetie, you don't have to pray. Just promise me you will look at it and just see what happens." She recalled her experience in her church at mass, describing the experience of discerning as "a gut feeling." Sara recalled, "It was like, you have got to go to GU, you just have to. Again, it just felt like that moment where Mary was telling me I love you, I love you. For some reason, this tabernacle, God was telling me you have to go to GU. I can't explain why but you do."[65]

When finally at Gonzaga, Sara felt somehow let down by God after a difficult first year at Gonzaga. She noted a visit to the church on Gonzaga's campus, "I wiped my face and went to the chapel and sat there and cried and was like what the hell. Tell me now. Why did you send me here? I don't understand . . . I am the most unhappy I have ever been in both my faith and just my personal life. You have got to give me a fucking answer. I was like I'm not going to leave this church until I get it. So you know 30 minutes go by and I'm like . . . where are you?"[66] Experiences with God can be both life giving and also frustrating. In seeking God, Sara

---

64. Green, personal interview, November 11, 2016.
65. Green, personal interview, November 11, 2016.
66. Green, personal interview, November 11, 2016.

joined the rank of many Christians before her, calling out to God in anguish.

Tristan Jones recalled his own spiritual experience with God, a time that has become clearer in reflection. Tristan, along with some friends, felt led by God to start a spiritual group on campus providing worship, prayer and spiritual encouragement for students. He recalled how God opened doors for him to begin a group on campus, "Through this men's small group, [we] . . . got the shared vision . . . to start [a worship night]. . . . At the end of freshmen year, we had been doing little acoustic guitar worship music sessions. The last part of the year was like 22 people. Just kind of these stepping stones of hey, we can do this. Sophomore year we . . . had this common space that we used for what we ended up calling Clay. And God took it over."[67] Tristan noted that people kept attending, and the community continued to develop and grow, becoming a place where he "made some of [his] closest friends."[68] Tristan Jones shared how the group continued to grow in number, inspiring other students to continue their night of worship. He noted that the new student leaders "have made it their own in really cool ways. We have gotten to go to some of them. That was a really cool way of seeing the patience and handy work of God."[69] Although beginning as something unknown, the group of students meeting snowballed into something bigger than the group of students that began the worship night.

April Garcia recalled that while at mass she regularly has a spiritual practice while praying for the Eucharist, upon listening to the Daily Bread in the prayer, she includes "a trait or characteristic that [she desires to] see in Jesus that [she] want[s] to try and replicate throughout the week."[70] Although many times she may forget she prayed for patience, or love during the week, she experienced God in a new way when she was feeling "very low

---

67. Jones, focus group interview, November 3, 2016.
68. Jones, focus group interview, November 3, 2016.
69. Jones, focus group interview, November 3, 2016.
70. Garcia, personal interview, November 12, 2016.

[and] was just feeling very defeated [and] tired."[71] April recalled, "When we were saying the prayer, I said the word acceptance and I don't even know where it came from. And I went to Eucharist and I just kept praying for acceptance. . . . I [didn't] even know why I [was] praying for this."[72]

Through a week of failure and disheartening news, April noted how she saw God at work in the little things, it "is actually a way of God showing me something that is higher than what I'm experiencing right now. . . . That is the first time I have felt a tangible, spiritual experience come from a series of events. Small events."[73] Spiritual experiences, both large and small, can bring confidence in forming spiritual identity and in helping students to own their faith. However, identity can continue to be confusing, particularly as students begin to seek congruence in all aspects of their life, including taking on leadership positions, exploring different styles of leadership, and developing a leadership identity.

---

71. Garcia, personal interview, November 12, 2016.
72. Garcia, personal interview, November 12, 2016.
73. Garcia, personal interview, November 12, 2016.

5

The Development of Leadership Identity

SPIRITUAL IDENTITY FORMATION AND leadership identity development do not appear to occur on simultaneous planes. For many student participants in this study, spirituality was introduced early in her or his life by parents, strongly influencing spiritual identity formation, along with church and parachurch mentors and peers. In comparison, leadership identity development was identified in students through some role modeling of parents, yet remained strongly personality driven and directly related to learning from courses, training and positional experience.

In examining leadership practices and explaining styles of leadership, students expressed both certainty and uncertainty in their leadership identity. Interestingly, in developing leadership identity, family remains a strong developmental influence. For example, some of the student participants have been told from an early age about their leadership capabilities and were asked to lead early on, while others pushed themselves and discovered their leadership capabilities along the way. In forming leadership identity, I will discuss Komives and coauthors' Leadership

Identity Development (LID) model, followed by styles of leadership, including authentic and vulnerable leadership and servant leadership.

Leadership Identity Development (LID) is based on a grounded theory study on leadership identity, answering the overarching questions: "How is leadership learned, and how is it developed as an aspect of personal or social identity over time?"[1] Komives, Owen, Longerbeam, Mainella, and Osteen defined leadership identity as "the cumulative confidence in one's ability to intentionally engage with others to accomplish group objectives."[2]

In the LID model, Komives and coauthors note that leadership identity itself progresses over six stages from awareness to exploration and engagement, then to leader identified, leadership differentiated, generativity, and finally to integration and synthesis (see table 1). Based on the LID research, Komives states, "College student leadership identity appears to be a developmental process that progresses from simple dependent leader-centric views of self with others to more complex interdependent views of leadership being non-positional and as a process among interdependent people. The developmental view of organizations shifts from organizations being hierarchical to organizations being complex systems both internally and externally in their relations to other organizations."[3] "Of interest . . . is that as students changed from being dependent on others (for example, being followers or being independent of others, for example, being positional leaders), they developed a consciousness of being interdependent with others."[4] In the cycle of the LID model, "each person discovers and uncovers their identity through a continual process of observation and reflection."[5]

1. Komives, "College Student Leadership Identity Development," 279.
2. Komives, Lucas, and McMahon, "Developing a Leadership Identity," 608.
3. Komives, "College Student Leadership Identity Development," 290.
4. Komives, "College Student Leadership Identity Development," 280–81.
5. Komives, Lucas, and McMahon, "Developing a Leadership Identity," 610.

In the LID model, stage one allows for a sense of awareness, and a recognition of leadership occurring around them through other individuals.[6] Stage two has individuals participating in leadership and contributing to a larger group. Stage three, leader identified, includes an individual managing people, accomplishing tasks, and following a hierarchical model and positional level of leadership. In the fourth stage, leadership differentiated, individuals experience a major transition of personal awareness, separating the individual from positional leadership, noting that all individuals can bring about change.

Stage	Leadership Dimensions
1. Awareness (Stage 1)	Leaders exist Leadership is external to self Individuals do not personally identify as a leader Individuals do not differentiate group roles
2. Exploration/Engagement (Stage 2)	Unfocused leadership Skill development and learning stage Intentional involvement in groups New responsibilities as a group member
3. Leader Identified (Stage 3)	Two phases: Emerging phase-try on leadership identity Immersion phase-live out leadership identity There are positional leaders and followers Leader is independent Leaders are responsible for outcomes

---

6. Komives et al., "Leadership Identity Model."

Stage	Leadership Dimensions
4. Leader Differentiated (Stage 4)	Two phases Emerging phase-try on leadership identity Immersion phase-live out leadership identity Leadership is not positional Leadership is interdependent Leadership is happening all around
5. Generativity (Stage 5)	Commit to larger purpose Personal passion based on beliefs and values Consider service as leadership activism Work toward social change Acknowledge interdependence Feel responsible for developing group members and sustaining organizations
6. Integration/Synthesis (Stage 6)	Continual and active engagement with leadership Grow in confidence Strive for congruence and integrity Understand "organizational complexity and practiced systematic thinking."[7] Adapt

Table 1. **Leadership Identity Dimensions**

Many of the participants in the Gonzaga study experienced a shift from stage three to stage four while in college. In the third stage, the leader identified; the group has identified leaders and followers, and in this hierarchical view, positional leaders are considered to be the individuals responsible for outcomes. Recognized for leadership potential or abilities, students are usually influenced by mentors such as teachers or parents particularly during this stage. The leader-differentiated, fourth stage, does not

7. Komives, Lucas, and McMahon, "Developing a Leadership Identity," 607.

view leadership as positional, but rather as interdependent on all group members. During this fourth stage, students recognize that leadership is happening all around them. All student participants reasoned that leadership is not positional, although some student leaders still struggled to put this belief into practice.

Two to three male participants still remained in stage three, two students who did not participate in leadership training at Gonzaga were in stage three, and a third participant struggled with leadership confidence, and went back and forth between recognizing himself as a leader. The remaining eleven participants had transitioned to stage four, leadership differentiated. In this stage, trust is developed within a group, and full participation, leadership and ideas exists among all group members. Students did not however, mention how their organization would continue following their departure from leadership or mention the desire to coach other student leaders. These areas are included in the transition to stage five. Participants did reference transitions toward passion for leadership, seeking a fit with the vision of the organization, and desiring to serve society and the common good.

No student participant expressed the generativity common to stage five, where a leader works to sustain the program and train others. The final and sixth stage integrates and synthesizes leadership into an individual's life, revealing a congruence of values and actions and a commitment to life-long learning and leadership development. These final stages may be more apparent in individuals who are employed in a position that lasts for longer than a year. Three of the fourteen participants had remained in a leadership position for more than one year. Many of the participants in the study held leadership positions that were shorter term, and did not have a sense of strategic planning as a part of his or her position. Another reason for students remaining in stages three and four may be developmental, and more common among emerging adults.

The LID model explains the development of leadership identity with multiple outlying developmental influences of adults, peers, meaningful involvement and reflective learning. Missing from the LID model is any spiritual identity component, which may fit in the categories of developing self and developmental influences. Within the cycle of leadership development, leadership identity is informed by internal group influences, developing self, changing view of self with others, and a broadening view of leadership. Komives and coauthors explain, the "developing self interacted with group influences to shape the student's changing view of self with others. This changing view of self in relation to others shaped the student's broadening view of what leadership is and created a leadership identity."[8] Although not to the degree of spiritual identity formation, parents and mentors did have a developmental influence on student leadership identity formation.

Factors in Leadership Identity

Among the students in the study, many grew in confidence based on parent modeling and feedback, and many of the students were initially prompted or asked to enter into leadership positions. According to Komives and coauthors, transitioning from the third stage to the fourth stage of the Leadership Identity Development model, the "mentoring role of adults and learning the language of leadership were critical" as was "expanding self-awareness," which is essential in each stage of transition.[9] Family and mentor relationships influence the building of leadership identity among participants and influences leadership style preferences.

Tristan Jones recalled the influence of his mother and her ability to be resilient under change. He noted how it was encouraging to see "her passions change . . . [and] see her put into a new environment."[10] He noted, "She loves it so much and it is super cool to watch it . . . that was such an inspiration for me."[11] Tristan also expressed the importance of seeing the compassion of his

8. Komives, Lucas, and McMahon, "Developing a Leadership Identity," 596.
9. Komives et al., "Leadership Identity Model," 414.
10. Jones, personal interview, November 11, 2016.
11. Jones, personal interview, November 11, 2016.

mother: "She does Big Brother-Big Sister and they highlighted her and her little sister [in a video]. That was really cool."[12] Henri Brown recalled the strong influence of his father in his own formation of leadership and leadership identity. Following a health scare from his father, Henri recalled how his dad remained filled with compassion and care for all those around him. "The whole time he was recovering he was like, how is your mom? His only request to me at the end of the three days was, take care of everybody else no matter what happens after this . . . I want my life to try to strive after that."[13] Parents provided a role modeled for their children in their behavior and actions, often informing the type of leadership their children desired to implement.

Parents can have a keen influence on the leadership development of college students. Lloyd White noted how his personality and the influence of his parents initially helped him to shape his leadership identity, "My parents have always described me as kind of just a . . . naturally born leader. Somebody who has always wanted to be up in front of people. That is what I thought it was for a long time. It was always about the position and just having—not power but . . . influence."[14] Henri Brown noted that his father told him that he was a leader, which helped to inform his leadership identity. "My dad is always [saying]—people watch you. . . . At your school people watch you. We had these conversations all the time."[15]

Along with parental mentoring, students that received words of encouragement were influenced to participate in leadership roles. Leadership confidence grew in male students when they received positions or were asked to lead. In fact, of the four male students participating in the one-on-one interviews, all four mentioned that they had been asked to lead, and that those incidents had been a significant deciding factor in their leadership efficacy. None of the female students mentioned being asked to lead.

12. Jones, personal interview, November 11, 2016.
13. Brown, personal interview, November 10, 2016.
14. White, personal interview, November 13, 2016.
15. Brown, personal interview, November 10, 2016.

Among male participants, each noted that a coach, principal, church member or family had asked them to take on a leadership role or formal position. Lloyd White remembered being asked to lead an 8th grade retreat as a junior in high school: "It was really cool to have siblings of my friends be there . . . [the] breakaway retreat and leading it was a huge turning point" in forming his identity and figuring out who he wanted to be.[16] Lloyd White noted, "I was really involved always in some sort of leadership role. I don't know, I was on ASB [Associated Student Body]. I was voted most involved in high school. It has just always been me."[17] He continued, "I have always gotten everything that I wanted . . . I have just always gotten [leadership positions] that have been harder to get. So I have never really truly lost."[18]

Liam Black found that from his time in high school playing sports, his coach "picked me and one other kid to be the leaders other team or the team captains. Which for me was just kind of awkward. I was fine with it."[19] His mother noted this instance, "Oh other people see the attributes that I see in him. They value that."[20]

Tristan Jones was asked to be a leader on his sporting team early on; "obviously coaches saw something in me that I didn't think I had. I think a lot of that was confidence. [I felt] I shouldn't be the leader cause maybe I was putting leadership as equating to ability or experience or performance. . . . I think [in] leadership there has to be an authenticity."[21] He also noted that in forming his identity, acceptance to a leadership program his first year gave him confidence: "I think it definitely was a process . . . being admitted to the program, [I decided], ok sure, I'm a leader."[22] One student participant in particular had a pattern of being asked to consider and take on leadership positions.

16. White, personal interview, November 13, 2016.
17. White, personal interview, November 13, 2016.
18. White, personal interview, November 13, 2016.
19. Black, personal interview, November 13, 2016.
20. Black, personal interview, November 13, 2016.
21. Jones, personal interview, November 11, 2016.
22. Jones, personal interview, November 11, 2016.

Unscripted Spirituality

Henri Brown discovered that throughout his life he has continually been asked to take on leadership positions, from church members, from family, and school leaders. He related, "I have thought a lot about this pattern a lot." Henri stated that the leadership positions, "[Are] not anything I searched for. I didn't press for those positions. I didn't even necessarily think about those positions until I was asked to do them. It was something that came to me in a way I didn't really expect and I was willing to say yes."[23] He recalled, "I had become the student body president of my high school . . . the principal asked me. I didn't necessarily decide to run for that role . . . by choice."[24] While volunteering with a non-profit organization, "I get this phone call going so our director of media quit . . . you are now formally the director of media. That was just the phone call."[25] In high school Henri found himself in a unique position as a Catholic student leader asked to organize Evangelical chapel speakers; "I love leadership positions. . . . So lo and behold, who is the chapel planning intern for the school? The one Catholic kid."[26]

In high school Henri Brown was also asked by his local parish priest to help lead a confirmation class he had just completed, and the following year was asked to lead the course alone. He recalled, "The Father of my parish . . . and the person in charge of catechism, they literally asked me after mass. . . . Since you taught [the class] last year, you want to teach the ones right before confirmation? . . . We want you to help teach the kids who are freshmen in high school. I literally did that a year ago. You want me to do what? And apparently they did and it worked out fine."[27] Sophomore year of college, Henri found himself in another leadership position through the prompting of others as a resident minister; "keep

---

23. Brown, personal interview, November 10, 2016.
24. Brown, personal interview, November 10, 2016.
25. Brown, personal interview, November 10, 2016.
26. Brown, personal interview, November 10, 2016.
27. Brown, personal interview, November 10, 2016.

in mind that before I applied, I didn't know where the university ministry office was."[28]

Along with mentoring, and influence, while at Gonzaga, student participants mentioned that their leadership identity shifted as they gained knowledge and training on leadership. In particular, many students participating in the Comprehensive Leadership Program (CLP) at Gonzaga exhibited greater vocabulary to discuss leadership concepts and styles than other participants. In helping to shape his leadership identity, Tristan noted that "the comprehensive leadership program has definitely taught me everyone is" a leader.[29] Student in this program also indicated a desire to empower other students and peers, acknowledging that leadership requires a group effort. Palmer describes a dark side of leadership as "functional atheism—the belief that ultimate responsibility for everything rests with me."[30] Students who had participated in cocurricular leadership training also exhibited strong leadership identity and development, yet articulated leadership theory and concepts to a lesser extent. Those student leaders with little leadership training tended toward positional and trait based descriptions of leadership, and did not have a full understanding of leadership theory and concepts. These same students with little or no leadership training did not express periods of leadership growth, indicating no awareness of varying leadership styles and had nominal self-awareness as a leader.

Gonzaga offers students leadership courses and training which helps develop a common language and understanding about leadership approaches and styles. Students that participated in these courses and even less informative trainings had a common language and approach to leadership and a greater leadership identity development. An additional step in developing greater leadership identity would provide guidance for congruence of personal values, such as spirituality and faith practice, with lived leadership experience.

28. Brown, personal interview, November 10, 2016.
29. Brown, personal interview, November 10, 2016.
30. Palmer, *Let Your Life Speak*, 88.

Unscripted Spirituality

A small minority of students indicated leadership experience played a large role in shaping their identities and growth. Lloyd White noted, "I think for me, having different leadership experiences has made me step out of my comfort zone, which has allowed me to grow and develop really."[31] According to Bandura, experiences are the "most influential source of efficacy information because they provide the most authentic evidence of whether one can muster what it takes to succeed."[32] Some of the most prominent styles of leadership that were emphasized and valued among student participants included servant leadership and authentic and vulnerable leadership.

Leadership as Spiritual Practice

As holistic people, who we are and what we do has the potential to impact our leadership. In the discussion on leadership with student participants, several characteristics emerged when discussing effective leadership styles. Students gravitated toward authentic and vulnerable leadership, and characteristics of servant leadership. At a time when students are still figuring out personal identity, interestingly, students gravitated toward the idea of leading with authenticity.

In college, students are often faced with the opportunity to be authentic or to put on a mask. Tristan Jones recalled the automatic responses of students around Gonzaga's campus: "I have found that there [are] conversation scripts, depending on the time of year, at least for walk-by conversations at Gonzaga."[33] Regularly, the conversation remains on the surface level: "How are you doing? Good. Good. How are you?"[34] Tristan noted, although "I am trying to be just a bit more intentional, even if I am asking how

---

31. White, personal interview, November 13, 2016.
32. Bandura, *Self-Efficacy*, 80.
33. Jones, personal interview, November 11, 2016.
34. Jones, personal interview, November 11, 2016.

are you?"³⁵ Tristan affirmed that listening is of utmost importance in creating intentionality with others, and paired with listening is personal vulnerability. Currently, as a leader, and person of faith, Tristan is "trying to work towards being a bit more candid with people as far as how my day is going to things I'm wrestling with God about and things."³⁶

Luthans and Avolio define authentic leadership as "a process that draws from both positive psychological capacities and a highly developed organizational context, which results in both greater self-awareness and self-regulated positive behaviors on the part of leaders and associates, fostering positive self-development."³⁷ Walumbwa and coauthors furthered the definition to include the following four components in authentic leadership: self-awareness, internalized moral perspective, balanced processing and relational transparency.³⁸ May and coauthors note that an authentic leader is: "confident, hopeful, optimistic, resilient, transparent, moral/ethical, future oriented, and gives priority to developing associates to be leaders."³⁹

Familiar with authentic leadership, many of the student participants posited that vulnerability and authenticity overflow from their faith and spiritual life. Lloyd White reasoned that in building relationships with people he leads, "I think a lot of faith and spiritual life includes authenticity and vulnerability."⁴⁰ Avolio and Gardner suggest that being congruent with one's values helps one be perceived as an authentic leader.⁴¹ Researchers have found positive relationships between authentic leadership and outcomes

---

35. Jones, personal interview, November 11, 2016.
36. Jones, personal interview, November 11, 2016.
37. Luthans and Avolio, "Authentic Leadership," 243. The concept of authentic leadership theory first appeared in Robert Terry's *Authentic Leadership* in 1993. Bill George later popularized the concept in his approachable business book *Authentic Leadership* in 2004.
38. Walumbwa et al., "Authentic Leadership."
39. May et al., "Developing the Moral Component," 243.
40. White, personal interview, November 13, 2016.
41. Avolio and Gardner, "Authentic Leadership Development."

such as trust, well-being, and organizational commitment.⁴² In discussing vulnerability in leadership and spirituality, Joy explained, "That is when the growth will happen, not just for your own personal spirituality, but [also] for your entire group. . . . I think if you have strong spirituality and you are vulnerable and able to talk about that or . . . have those vulnerable moments growing together, your end product, whatever that is—whether it is a class project or a ministry or something—it is going to be so much stronger and more genuine. More genuinely reflective of what you wanted it to be anyway."⁴³

Sara Green explained that her spirituality and Catholic faith impacts how she views all people, and relates to the people she leads, "I feel like as a part of the Catholic faith, we all believe that every person is in God's dignity and respect. So that gives you this mindset of I really need to look out for those who are struggling, rather than just this why are you struggling. So, when you are maybe helping someone or criticizing them, even in a positive way . . . it still comes from this genuine care for them as an individual, not just someone who is under your leadership."⁴⁴ According to Parker Palmer, "The power for authentic leadership . . . is found not in external arrangements but in the human heart. Authentic leaders in every setting—from families to nation-states—aim at liberating the heart, their own and others', so that its powers can liberate the world."⁴⁵ Students made this connection, by referring to authentic leadership and the need to live vulnerably before the people that they are leading.

April Garcia said that in forming her personal definition of leadership, she believes "the best leaders are the ones that are able to admit their weaknesses."⁴⁶ Sara Green noted, "I think as leaders,

---

42. Gardner et al., *Authentic Leadership Theory*; Hunt et al., "Leader Emotional Displays"; Jensen and Luthans, "Entrepreneurs as Authentic Leaders"; Peus et al., "Authentic Leadership."

43. Smith, focus group interview, November 3, 2016.

44. Green, focus group interview, November 4, 2016.

45. Palmer, *Let Your Life Speak*, 76.

46. Garcia, personal interview, November 12, 2016.

we forget to allow ourselves weakness. We always feel like, if I'm a leader I have got to be the strongest one[s] all the time. . . . Some of the most admirable people I have ever met have been the people who have let me see their weakest moments. They have taught me so much through that."[47] In authentic leadership theory, authenticity is viewed as being rooted in action that is "both true and real in ourselves and in the world."[48] To be an authentic leader that can help others through "major ups and major downs," she notes that in leading, "I want you to see the downs. I want you to know how to get through yours. . . . I think that is something we don't remind ourselves of—the value of weakness."[49]

During her leadership role on campus, Joy Smith noted how her leadership improved by building intentional relationships with those she was leading, and by a vulnerable leader. She acknowledged, "I think one thing I have learned this year in leadership positions I'm in, mainly from my mentors . . . is you don't have to be the leader that has it all together. And honestly, even in our classes we talked a little bit about this. . . . If you don't have it all together and you show it to the people you are leading, it is going to have such a strong impact."[50]

Jessie Gray noted that at times, authentic leaders can scare us because of our own fragility: "I think it is important to just be honest about where you are because I remember . . . that Mother Theresa went through . . . 10 years or something where she didn't believe in God. . . . That is just mind blowing to me because she is obviously a phenomenal person. Had such a beautiful heart and faith. You know, just changed so many people's lives. So, to hear that kind of . . . jars me. What does that mean for the rest of us?"[51]

Yet, Jessie Gray took away the importance of learning about weaknesses in leaders, such as doubts in faith. She noted that the honesty mother Teresa shared is important, "It validates this year

47. Green, personal interview, November 4, 2016.
48. Terry, *Authentic Leadership*, 111–12.
49. Terry, *Authentic Leadership*, 111–12.
50. Smith, focus group interview, November 3, 2016.
51. Gray, personal interview, November 12, 2016.

where I was like, what is my faith right now? I think that I would feel worse and more shameful and weaker about those parts of me if other people weren't honest about that."[52] Lloyd White highlighted the importance of modeling vulnerability in leading on campus. He recalled a time he was able to be vulnerable with fellow students. During an event on campus, Lloyd was able to share his experience with his peers while "also meeting people where they were at in their stories. I guess showing people that they are not alone."[53] In highlighting his personal story, Lloyd encouraged his peers, and provided a safe space for other students to be authentic and vulnerable. In doing so, Lloyd was seeking to serve his community.

Scholars have attempted to measure authentic leadership using multiple scales, from the perspective of supervisors, followers, and individuals interested in self-assessment. Using samples from China, Kenya, and the United States, Walumbwa and coauthors found that authentic leadership was a major indicator for balanced processing, internalized moral perspective, self-awareness, and relational transparency, with positive correlations with ethical and transformational leadership.[54]

Regardless of the training received at Gonzaga or the desire to be authentic as leaders, many student leaders that participated in this study struggled to connect their spiritual practice in the context of spiritual leadership. This is reflected in participants' LID stage three and four, whereas congruence of values and praxis are implemented in the sixth stage. Bill George presents leadership as necessarily integrated with spirituality; he asserts, "Leaders are defined by their values and their character. The values of the authentic leader are shaped by personal beliefs, developed through study, introspection, and consultation with others—and a lifetime

---

52. Gray, personal interview, November 12, 2016.

53. White, personal interview, November 13, 2016.

54. Walumbwa and coauthors created the Authentic Leadership Questionnaire (ALQ), a qualitative questionnaire, including sixteen items grouped in categories of: self-awareness, relational transparency, internalized moral perspective, and balanced processing.

The Development of Leadership Identity

experience."[55] Interestingly, these same student participants were in the process of practicing spirituality in their leadership, and expressed themselves and their spirituality by leading relationally, authentically, with vulnerability, and in serving their peers.

Similar to authentic and vulnerable leadership, the characteristics of servant leadership discussed by Robert Greenleaf[56] and outlined by Spears[57] are highly relational. Servant leadership is a philosophy based on the writings and leadership experience of Robert Greenleaf. Greenleaf defined servant leadership as those leaders who are "servant first. . . . It begins with the natural feeling that one wants to serve, to serve first. Then conscious choice brings one to aspire to lead."[58] In other words, servant leaders seek to lead in such a way that they are able to positively influence their peers, employers, and coworkers in order to "raise the human spirit."[59] Although based on the working knowledge of Greenleaf, an organizational executive working with adults, servant leadership has been highly influential in the development of relational and reciprocal student leadership theories.

During the interviews, I observed if students mentioned servant leadership characteristics of self-awareness, along with the characteristics of listening, empathy, building community, and a commitment to the growth of people. Many of the student leaders at Gonzaga University received training in servant leadership; therefore, it was interesting to note that those students that received training were able to articulate their connection with servant leadership. The students also indicated practicing servant leadership characteristics of listening, empathy and commitment to the growth of people.

---

55. George, *Authentic Leadership*, 20.

56. Greenleaf published his influential work *The Servant as Leader* in 1970.

57. Larry Spears explained the importance of nurturing the characteristics of listening, empathy, healing, awareness, persuasion, conceptualization, foresight, stewardship, commitment to the growth of people, and building community in the development of Servant Leaders.

58. Greenleaf, *Servant as Leader*, 27.

59. Greenleaf, *Servant as Leader*, 185.

In discussing leadership practices, some of the student participants explicitly referred to servant leadership as an inspiration for their leadership style. For example, Henri Brown noted that his desire to volunteer leading in his organization was inspired from a desire to serve his peers, noting it is "a chance for me to give back."[60] Joy Smith also shared that she has come to a point in her leadership where she "feel[s] like leadership as an honor" and that she "will do everything [she] can to serve."[61]

One of the positive side effects of servant leadership is that those who lead may multiply their efforts by influencing others toward a healthy, judicious, service-oriented lifestyle. Servant leaders also look at bringing healing and growth to those they serve by "helping others to a larger and nobler vision and purpose than they would be likely to attain for themselves."[62] Spears commented, "Servant leaders believe that people have an intrinsic value.... As such, the servant leader is deeply committed to the growth of each and every individual within his or her organization."[63]

After taking her first Comprehensive Leadership Program (CLP) course at Gonzaga, April Garcia noted her movement away from her original definition a leader as personality based with loud and energetic qualities, toward an empathetic servant leader. She explained her style of leadership: "This mixture of servant leadership and being authentic and using the things you really love and the talents that you are really good at in a way that is going to help other people feel included and in a way that is going to be beneficial for more people than just the leader themselves."[64] She explained, "The best leaders are the ones that people don't even see doing the work. Because, the work that you are doing behind the scenes is the work that is actually going to make the biggest difference."[65] Servant Leadership is not a quick fix for student lead-

60. Brown, personal interview, November 10, 2016.
61. Smith, personal interview, November 10, 2016.
62. Greenleaf, *Servant as Leader*, 240.
63. Spears, "Character and Servant Leadership," 29.
64. Garcia, personal interview, November 12, 2016.
65. Garcia, personal interview, November 12, 2016.

ers, but is slow and deliberate work. Don Frick explained it well when he observes, "Rewarding, challenging, risky growth is often uncomfortable and seldom neat. Servant leadership simply is not easy. Most meaningful things seldom are."[66]

Although not using language explicitly referring to servant leadership, Liam Black noted the futility of self-serving leadership, "What is the point of the business? Are you trying to make doors? Ok sweet. That is not really fun at all. But if you are doing it with a purpose to give back to the community or help a family or help your next-door neighbor or somebody struggling, then you have a higher purpose. And all of a sudden building doors means something."[67] Liam Black noted that by serving others in leadership and in developing a business that looks for the greater common good, "there is value to it and you have a purpose besides self-interest" and "that is how I have tied [my] spirituality into" leading.[68] Henri Brown shared that from his family's' example, "I have learned that other people matter before me. . . . It is my job to help love and care for others first. That kind of perspective . . . that love has to be the center of all that you do."[69]

Participants in the study recalled characteristics of servant leadership that they practice. Jill Kind recalled a book she read on servant leadership that she connected to her spirituality and faith. She noted that in leading and being a servant leader, she desired the growth of her peers, a key characteristic of servant leadership: "You have to realize that with your position it is not about you, it is about the group you are leading. . . . Leadership is loving one another, not an emotion or a feeling, but more like meeting people's needs, not necessarily their wants, but their needs. What they truly need . . . is not always the easiest thing. But in the end it helps them grow."[70] Sara Green explained that in her workplace, she likewise desires to empower her peers, "We had a coworker

66. Frick, afterword to "Understanding Robert K. Greenleaf," 358.
67. Black, focus group interview, November 4, 2016.
68. Black, focus group interview, November 4, 2016.
69. Brown, personal interview, November 10, 2016.
70. Kind, focus group interview, November 3, 2016.

who he is one of our best [workers]. No one can say no to him and we need people like that. He got this amazing job offer and intern opportunity. And as much as [I] . . . would love to say please stay, I also think about his future and what he is working hard towards. I think to myself—but that is what you need to go after."[71]

In practicing servant leadership, Joy Smith noted the importance of listening to the people she leads: "I make sure to hear everything first and include everyone in a group conversation and then I try to acknowledge all of that before I move to a solution."[72] According to Spears, "Listening, coupled with periods of reflection, is essential to the growth and well-being of the servant leader."[73] However, it cannot be assumed that because an individual is competent and kind that they are able to serve and lead others well, or know how to listen.[74] April Garcia noted the importance of empowering her followers as well as listening. April recognized a need to "let other people take the reins and have louder voices than me."[75] She acknowledged the opportunity to learn from her peers "if I'm quiet in situations or if I just listen or have that special awareness."[76] April reiterated that the best leaders listen first, "allowing everyone in the room to have an equal part and equal participation in what they want to do."[77]

Similarly, Tristan Jones noted the impact of his developing concept of leadership from a servant leadership class with CLP: "With servant leadership—to lead, you must first serve."[78] He connected this to his own experience in serving his peers: "For a month I worked at a camp, a Young Life camp as a food server. . . . I wanted to give back because it had been such a foundational time

---

71. Green, focus group interview, November 4, 2016.
72. Smith, personal interview, November 10, 2016.
73. Spears, "Character and Servant Leadership," 27.
74. Greenleaf, *Servant Leadership*, 314.
75. Garcia, personal interview, November 12, 2016.
76. Garcia, personal interview, November 12, 2016.
77. Garcia, personal interview, November 12, 2016.
78. Jones, personal interview, November 11, 2016.

for me in my faith life."[79] He continued, "I feel like that is where I saw prayer at work and realized ministry and God's work can be something as simple as bringing your food to you. So that was seeing God in a new way."[80]

The dimensions of the spiritual formation model in figure 2 overlap with the philosophy of servant leadership, particularly in the outward expression of service and leadership. Greenleaf was a practicing Quaker, a Christian man informed by the service and leadership of Christ, and in congruence with Greenleaf's Christian values and principles, servant leadership displays a Christian emphasis of service. Within the Christian faith Jesus acts as a humble leader, serving his followers, directly linking service as leadership. An example of this is found in John 13:1–17, where Jesus washes the feet of the disciples, the act of a servant, not of a powerful king, or even teacher. Similar to the modeling of Christ for his disciples, Greenleaf's test of a servant leader includes the fruit of healthy followers: "Do those served grow as persons? Do they, while being served, become healthier, wiser, freer, more autonomous, more likely themselves to become servants? And, what is the effect on the least privileged in society? Will they benefit or at least not be further deprived?"[81]

In practicing leadership styles, students indicated the importance of relational characteristics of servant leadership, along with authenticity and vulnerability, noting the spiritual motivation for their leadership styles. Students also mentioned that they transitioned between the stages of leadership identity development mostly through the study of new leadership theoretical frameworks. Periods of transition in leadership development were instrumental in moving participants toward the next stage of learning and leading. Transitions are also a natural part of the college experience, and can bring about periods of personal and spiritual growth.

---

79. Jones, personal interview, November 11, 2016.
80. Jones, personal interview, November 11, 2016.
81. Greenleaf, *Servant Leadership*, 27.

6

The Role of Transitions and Suffering

IN THE MIDST OF suffering or transition, individuals can experience confusion, isolation, and a lack of hope. Eugene Peterson explained the mystery of suffering in the life of a Christian, "For many, the first great surprise of the Christian life is in the form of troubles we meet. Somehow it is not what we had supposed: we had expected something quite different; we had our minds set on Eden or on New Jerusalem. We are rudely awakened to something very different."[1] Yet interestingly, suffering and transition can often serve as a catalyst for personal growth and spiritual resilience.

College is often described as a period of time for learning, self-growth and exploration, an essential milestone toward adulthood filled with wonderful memories and adventure. However, for many undergraduate students in North America, college is filled with confusing transitions, or life changes, that bring about periods of discomfort and isolation. Student participants mentioned that during their transitionary periods during college, such as their first semester at college, or during experiences abroad, or even returning back to campus, they experienced periods of distress where

---

1. Peterson, *Long Obedience*, 38–39.

they were rocked to their core. These students found themselves out of their comfort zones, in places where they no longer had a strong sense of community, or support, or self.

Suffering in Transition

During her transition to college three years ago, Joy Smith experienced one of the lowest periods of her life. She found herself torn between drinking with friends underage, engaging with people, and being honest with herself, noting: "I think there [was] a disconnect, 'I'm not being who I am.'"[2] "It is hard too when I think now I'm finally getting to the point where I can like balance these two worlds. . . . They shouldn't be two worlds."[3] She felt that she was not truly being herself. She explained, "I got documented a couple times. I was not being the person that I thought I was or that I knew I was. Everyone who knew me here thought I was a different person than I knew I was because of what I was doing; because of the person I was presenting myself to be. . . . It was hard to face . . . [and] realize I had been wrong in all these things."[4] She noted that relationally, "I didn't really have the support in my friend group because I hadn't sought out the right friends for that."[5] These friends "weren't really pushing me to grow in my faith or my leadership or anything really."[6] She also connected her feeling of disconnection with her lack of involvement. Joy recollected her years at Gonzaga: "I feel like freshmen year I wasn't in leadership positions and that is when I was really low. Then sophomore year I felt like I was in a position where I was meant to be and I was feeling great. And then junior year I kind of didn't have that position. I didn't have that base again."[7]

2. Smith, personal interview, November 10, 2016.
3. Smith, personal interview, November 10, 2016.
4. Smith, personal interview, November 10, 2016.
5. Smith, personal interview, November 10, 2016.
6. Smith, personal interview, November 10, 2016.
7. Smith, personal interview, November 10, 2016.

Unscripted Spirituality

When explaining why she lived in between two worlds, Joy noted, "I definitely took it too far because I don't think I had the foundations I had grown up with in my leadership positions and my involvement. I didn't have that to remind me—that is not what you . . . do."[8] Yet not all students experience their first semester of college as a period of suffering.

In contrast, upon moving to Gonzaga his first year of college, Tristan Jones felt he could be fully himself. He contemplated this transition period: "Maybe that is because I had friends from high school or maybe [I] blossom[ed] more into myself and was comfortable with the person I felt like I was and was becoming."[9] Relationships with peers with similar values attributed to a sense of self for Tristan. Lloyd White likewise noted that in transitioning to his first year in college he felt like he had a "support system in place."[10] Lloyd noted that this support system came from developing friendships with "people who wanted to do the same thing as me . . . wanting to find a church home, wanting to be in community and relationships with others and chasing after the same things. It was really, really cool."[11] Relationships with peers in college became a support system for these students, helping them to transition to college easily, and to retain their sense of identity.

April Garcia pronounced her study abroad experience as "the single most uncomfortable experience of my entire life."[12] She recalled, "There would be these days that you would wake up feeling great and you would go out into the community and you would just mess up something so bad with their culture. Just put your head down and walk back into your room and be like I can't believe I did that. I was so hard on myself there. Harder on myself than I have ever been. I'm not a big crier and I was crying every day because I was just so mad."[13] The complexity of living in a different culture,

---

8. Smith, personal interview, November 10, 2016.
9. Jones, personal interview, November 11, 2016.
10. White, personal interview, November 13, 2016.
11. White, personal interview, November 13, 2016.
12. Garcia, focus group interview, November 4, 2016.
13. Garcia, focus group interview, November 4, 2016.

being in new surroundings and not having an established network for support can be disconcerting and painful.

These periods of transition, although at times uncomfortable, can also bring about times of personal and spiritual growth. A part of the issue living abroad, April noted, is coming to terms with oneself and one's imperfections, which can eventually lead to greater self-knowledge. She explained, "I think being uncomfortable and making mistakes in that setting that was so unfamiliar ... helped me to realize that you can't be perfect in everything that you do and that those imperfections are what shape you and what give you your individuality and your unique traits."[14] Like April, Jessie Gray and Tristan Jones shared their study abroad experiences as critical moments of disconnection and for spiritual reflection.

Exposure to new belief practices and new cultures left Jessie Gray feeling uncomfortable and out of place. She found her abroad experience to be challenging for two main reasons: "I wasn't really being supported and then there were just a lot of people who had very different ideas about how to live than me. Whether it was people in my program or people where I was" living.[15] According to Astin and coauthors, "Studying abroad, discussing religion, and community service enlarge students' perspectives in countless ways by exposing them to a diversity of peoples, ideas, and cultures. Among many other things, such experiences allow students to reflect on what they have in common with others. While encountering such differences helps students to examine preconceived notions and beliefs about self and other, it also lets them recognize their oneness with others and the world."[16]

While abroad, developing relationships with like-minded people can be difficult for many students. Jessie Gray noted that among her peers abroad, "a lot of people in my group liked to go out and drink a lot. . . . Even if you are in Southern Africa, people are going to find ways to make that happen."[17] The drinking be-

14. Garcia, focus group interview, November 4, 2016.
15. Gray, personal interview, November 12, 2016.
16. Astin et al., *Cultivating the Spirit*, 80.
17. Gray, personal interview, November 12, 2016.

Unscripted Spirituality

havior of her peers distressed Jessie. She explained, "I was kind of questioning the greater humanity . . . so even the people that are . . . deciding to apply for this intense program abroad are still choosing this? What? It just was pretty mind blowing to me to try to figure that out."[18] She questioned their motives of serving and learning abroad in this community: "Why are you doing this?" She instead chose to "hang out with [her] host family."[19]

A part of the discomfort comes from being outside of a familiar place, exposed to new ways of living, and developing a growing awareness of your culture and beliefs in new ways. For Jessie Gray she struggled with regular concerns shared by many college students who travel to developing countries, like "seeing people that are in extreme poverty and extreme suffering."[20] She didn't quite know "what to even say to someone who is in that situation."[21] She noted, "I felt useless and I was like why am I even here? I paid all this money for a plane ticket and I'm paying for this program and do people here just see me as some rich white girl that is going to steal from."[22]

Another element of distress for Jessie Gray was feeling "harassed all the time" by men while "walking through the bus station."[23] This element of harassment raised questions for Jessie, "Why am I here? Where are the people that understand me?"[24] Jessie Gray noted that while abroad, "I had this spiritual dry spell" and found herself to be "very distracted" from her spiritual practices and faith values.[25] She explained, "There wasn't really an obvious place for me to [do yoga] while I was abroad but I wasn't doing it at all . . . I was journaling some but not like regularly. I am all about community and I didn't really have a distinct spiritual

18. Gray, personal interview, November 12, 2016.
19. Gray, personal interview, November 12, 2016.
20. Gray, personal interview, November 12, 2016.
21. Gray, personal interview, November 12, 2016.
22. Gray, personal interview, November 12, 2016.
23. Gray, personal interview, November 12, 2016.
24. Gray, personal interview, November 12, 2016.
25. Gray, personal interview, November 12, 2016.

community there. I didn't have a [Christian Life Community] kind of thing . . . I didn't have a regular church I was going to."[26]

Although in spiritual crisis while abroad, Jessie was proactive, visiting different churches, and joining the Campus Crusade parachurch organization. She noted, that connecting with the organization was "a good spiritual thing for me there."[27] After Jessie figured out that she needed spiritual support, and she "wasn't really being supported by anyone else spiritually," she began "reaching out to [her] youth director, which eventually [made] the last few months . . . really good."[28]

Jessie Gray intentionally engaged with different faith practices while abroad, attending many different styles of churches. She noted "that was really neat to observe from a cultural perspective," yet some of her experiences were also unsettling. She recalled, "I had one church I had a demon cast out of me. I was like ok. I didn't choose this. . . . I didn't feel any different. . . . It is not the way that I practice my religion. It is not the way I believe, so I think it didn't have the same spiritual impact on me as it would someone who is Pentecostal. A lot of what these churches are."[29] In retrospect, Jessie noted, "It was really interesting. Just like culturally and spiritually to go to these different churches and see what a Lutheran church in Botswana looks like and . . . Pentecostal. . . . To go to like 4-hour church services. It is crazy."[30] Along with being exposed to different churches, Jessie also came into contact with many friends abroad that raised new questions of her own faith and spiritual beliefs. Jessie recalled that although in the moment not sharing similar values and beliefs was difficult, in retrospect, the experience opened new doors: "My closest friends there were not religious or were of different faith backgrounds, which ended

---

26. Gray, personal interview, November 12, 2016.
27. Gray, personal interview, November 12, 2016.
28. Gray, personal interview, November 12, 2016.
29. Gray, personal interview, November 12, 2016.
30. Gray, personal interview, November 12, 2016.

Unscripted Spirituality

up being really good for me because now I am really involved in faith work and really excited about that."[31]

While Jessie Gray was living abroad, she experienced a great sense of belonging and spiritual connection during an all-day funeral service. She recalled waking early, attending a vigil, and singing and standing the entire time.[32] Although she did not know the language, or even the man who had died, Jessie still felt deeply moved and deeply spiritual.[33] She recalled viewing a group of elderly people standing and singing, "There was a lot of sadness and a lot of despair, but there was also a lot of celebration. . . . I remember just closing my eyes for a long time. More than I maybe would be comfortable with usually. Just really trying to absorb that moment because it was so [moving], even visually, this circle of people around this grave. . . . Even these 80-year-old people are like shoveling dirt . . . because they all love this person."[34]

Jessie continued to explain that the funeral served as "something where I could really feel that everyone was really present there. It was a really meaningful experience."[35] Central to the funeral experience for Jessie, was that she "didn't feel like an outsider" but was welcomed to participate in the community. She related that being different and alone was "something that was really hard and exhausting for me," yet in this shared experience at the funeral she belonged.[36] Spiritual belonging, and building relationships can often make the difference for college students between despair or growth.

Tristan Jones noted the difficulty of doing faith alone while he was abroad. He recalled, "Since the beginning of my faith I have been in groups. So for the first time I was alone in that."[37] Tristan Jones noted that culturally, the country he was living in felt

31. Gray, personal interview, November 12, 2016.
32. Gray, personal interview, November 12, 2016.
33. Gray, personal interview, November 12, 2016.
34. Gray, personal interview, November 12, 2016.
35. Gray, personal interview, November 12, 2016.
36. Gray, personal interview, November 12, 2016.
37. Jones, personal interview, November 11, 2016.

like "more of a secular place. Especially the campus" he was on.[38] Tristan explained that the interests of the other students living on his campus did not connect with him personally. He recalled, "A lot of the priorities of the other Americans and my flat-mates were partying. There was that whole different dynamic of [legality]. We are 18."[39] Building relationships with new peers while abroad can be a difficult, as can navigating the relational dynamics of the host nation while living in a new cultural setting. Tristan Jones recognized that going abroad, I "still felt true to who I was . . . day to day, interacting with people . . . but then [I wasn't] investing in [my] faith so [I wasn't] all there."[40]

Tristan directly tied his mental, emotional and spiritual health with a need for spiritual support, and intentionality while abroad. Tristan Jones explained that the lack of spiritual care while abroad influenced him spiritually, "[I] loved my experience abroad but . . . I really ran myself into the ground because I wasn't doing self-care and pouring or filling my cup back up."[41] Tristan explained, "I was surrounded by people, so I wasn't alone, but still, [I] felt more alone. . . . I didn't have this part, the spiritual part of my life that I was speaking about."[42] He attempted to connect with his peers spiritually, and attempted to have conversations: "I talked with my British flat-mates a few times because they saw my Young Life water bottle and were like what is that? . . . But that is more where the conversation ended."[43] He attempted to connect spiritually to a new church community, yet found himself distracted: "[I] went to church once over there at Hillsong, which is big. But cool. Checked that out. But yeah I just wasn't really being intentional in taking the things like I needed to stay healthy spiritually and emotionally cause there were lots of new people. Everyone is new

---

38. Jones, personal interview, November 11, 2016.
39. Jones, personal interview, November 11, 2016.
40. Jones, personal interview, November 11, 2016.
41. Jones, personal interview, November 11, 2016.
42. Jones, personal interview, November 11, 2016.
43. Jones, personal interview, November 11, 2016.

Unscripted Spirituality

there. Tons of new sites. I feel like that kept me going. That was kind of my fuel. . . . Let's have fun."[44]

Following a busy first few weeks, Tristan Jones began to struggle with depression while abroad. He noted that once travel slowed down, he "just didn't really have the energy to get out of bed" and "wasn't in a great spot mentally."[45] He recalled, "It kind of became normal and I was . . . halfway through maybe two or three weeks into just feeling—knowing I was in a bad place but just wallowing in it. . . . It was kind of like a rock bottom."[46]

Tristan Jones recognized, "I was in this new, hard space that didn't look like the intentional community I had been with since sophomore year of high school. But you can still recreate parts of that."[47] Tristan asked of himself: "Why aren't you doing the things that brought you life before?"[48] He noted the need for intentionality in taking "my emotional health [and] my spiritual health back into my hands. . . . I was more intentional as far as getting back into reading the Bible or just reading. I feel like that is such a therapeutic activity in itself."[49]

After an unexpected return to Gonzaga following her time abroad, Jessie Gray recalled her "strange transition" back to campus: "I ended up just living with one person who I didn't know because all my friends already had housing. And then I was trying to adjust to American culture. . . . I didn't have any leadership positions in that spring . . . I do put a lot of my identity and I pride myself in being in positions where I get to lift other people up. I was feeling pretty low and then I wasn't lifting anyone else up."[50]

Returning to Gonzaga following her time abroad, April Garcia suggested, "I went through some really bad, post-traveling depression. I think it came just from that first world guilt and also

---

44. Jones, personal interview, November 11, 2016.
45. Jones, personal interview, November 11, 2016.
46. Jones, personal interview, November 11, 2016.
47. Jones, personal interview, November 11, 2016.
48. Jones, personal interview, November 11, 2016.
49. Jones, personal interview, November 11, 2016.
50. Gray, personal interview, November 12, 2016.

... recognizing so many things about myself."[51] She continued, "I just never really recognized those things until after coming home from such a shocking experience.... Just this whole storm within myself."[52]

Joy Smith likewise, experienced a disconnection from her time abroad with her return to Gonzaga's campus: "I didn't have any leadership positions... because I had been gone first semester. So that was a struggle getting back into it."[53] Yet, she quickly addressed her feeling of disconnection by becoming more involved, "I was realizing that my senior year I need to make the full use of this last year and I think maybe that is when I realized that I feel most confident and comfortable at home and like I'm growing when I'm in a position of leadership where I feel like I am meant to be in."[54] Faced with new cultures, people, and situations, many students are unable to process all of the different emotions and experiences while abroad. Some of the participants mentioned, that while abroad, they were unable to recognize their need for assistance. Jessie noted that during her experience abroad, "I think it was something that I didn't even really realize that my time abroad was a spiritual low until this summer. Because I had a blast while I was there.... I think I was internalizing a lot of those little negative experiences and just kind of brushing them off."[55]

Jessie initially explained away her spiritual discomfort as a cultural issue, "That is how things happen here... I am just going to have to get used to his, I'm going to have to accept this."[56] With reflection, Jessie argued that her spiritual discomfort was genuinely tied to spiritual struggle, and a lack of spiritual support. "The thesis of social constructivism is that our minds do not mirror experience or reality. Rather, our minds project and reconstitute

---

51. Garcia, personal interview, November 12, 2016.
52. Garcia, personal interview, November 12, 2016.
53. Smith, personal interview, November 10, 2016.
54. Smith, personal interview, November 10, 2016.
55. Gray, personal interview, November 12, 2016.
56. Gray, personal interview, November 12, 2016.

experience."[57] In reconstituting her experience, Jessie was able to process her period of spiritual dryness while abroad, and find clarity in her suffering, bringing about a period of self-awareness and growth.

The Sustaining Work of the Holy Spirit

In the Christian faith tradition, suffering is a consistent theme throughout Scripture and in theological discussion. In Romans 4:1–8 the Apostle Paul discusses the paradox of suffering, linking it with growth, and the hope found in Christ: "Therefore since we have been justified through faith, we have peace through our Lord Jesus Christ, through whom we have gained access by faith into this grace in which we now stand. And we boast in the hope of the glory of God. Not only so, but we also glory in our sufferings, because we know that suffering produces perseverance; perseverance, character; and character, hope. And hope does not put us to shame, because God's love has been poured out into our hearts through the Holy Spirit, who has been given to us." In the midst of suffering, participants discussed periods of time where they were crushed and affected emotionally and spiritually. Yet in reflection many of the participants recognized that they had grown and come through the other side with stronger confidence in God and their spiritual identity.

Ignatius of Loyola, the founder of the Jesuit order, or Society of Jesus, wrote the Spiritual Exercises, a compilation of prayers, meditations and contemplative practices focused on the life and journey of Christ. In the Spiritual Exercises, Ignatius describes the Christian faith in terms of periods of consolation and desolation.[58] He explains desolation as those things that agitate or disturb, that discourages individuals or keeps them from God, while consolation instead quietly and gently leads an individual toward peace and joy, and toward loving God. The Christian journey requires a

---

57. Werhane et al., "Social Constructivism," 106.
58. Ignatius of Loyola and Puhl, *Spiritual Exercises of Saint Ignatius*, 1.

long obedience,[59] with the end goal of a life worth living, filled with complexity, and the paradox of joy in the midst of suffering.

In reflecting on life's challenges, student participants made an interesting connection between their struggle and spiritual strengthening. Often, during times of difficulties students also experienced the presence of God profoundly, or in retrospect, students recall a new maturity that has come out of their time of suffering. Joy Smith recalled, following a difficult time, "I don't know if I have ever felt closer to God or more spiritual internally settled, even though I was questioning."[60] Sharon Parks argued, "A worthy faith must bear the test of lived experience in the real world—our discoveries and disappointments, expectations and betrayals, assumptions and surprises. It is in the ongoing dialogue between self and world, between community and lived reality, that meaning—a faith—takes form."[61] Although suffering was never considered to be a positive occurrence, in retrospect, student participants exclaimed that a positive outcome of suffering was often spiritual growth.

Lloyd White noted the connection between suffering and profound spiritual experience; "I think for me, some of the highest points in my spiritual life, whether I would like to believe it or not, are during kind of the darker times."[62] He explained, noting that after people go through difficult times, or hit rock bottom, faith "means more, because you have had to go through those struggles and suffering" even if you "wish that it wouldn't be that way."[63]

Henri Brown described the period of stress and suffering he experienced during college in terms of the Jesuit notion of desolation, a movement away from God. According to Álvarez, "God

---

59. Nietzsche wrote in *Beyond Good and Evil*, "The essential thing in heaven and earth is . . . that there should be long obedience in the same direction; there thereby results, and has always resulted in the long run, something which has made life worth living" (188).

60. Smith, focus group interview, November 3, 2016.

61. Parks, *Big Questions, Worthy Dreams*, 23.

62. White, focus group interview, November 3, 2016.

63. White, focus group interview, November 3, 2016.

encounters human beings in the totality of their reality and generates within them an echo that is mainly of an affective nature. The echo takes the form of feelings that Ignatius calls movements of consolation or desolation."[64] Henri recalled hearing shocking news from his family about a family member's poor health during his first year of college, noting, "My world was changed forever."[65] He continued, "In the moment I was crushed . . . because I hadn't earned the responsibility being placed on me. I wasn't in a lot of ways ready for [this responsibility]. . . . [But] I didn't have a choice."[66]

During this period of desolation Henri explained, "I had nightmares for easily the last year about things that happened. Situations that I didn't want to think about in my own life. . . . I was in a state of constant depression and desolation spiritually."[67] Henri noted that even three years later, he couldn't recall everything that happened during that time-period. "I blotted it out. To me personally, I choose not to think about that time because I was in such bad place."[68] Unprepared for the effects of a heavy responsibility, as well as the loss and suffering he faced, Henri related his experience of the Jesuit concept of consolation, a movement toward God. In the midst of suffering, Henri found peace. He noted the presence of God imbuing him with His words and strength, as well as the unforeseen joy of walking with his family in new ways. "I watched my super hero be a super hero in a way I hadn't been expecting. It was a different kind of death. That is the retrospective."[69]

During this time, Henri observed that the Holy Spirit was giving him the energy and strength to do what he needed to do: "I think that is that physical example of something else getting me through that period because I wasn't sustaining myself."[70] The

64. Álvarez, "Promotion of Justice," 12.
65. Álvarez, "Promotion of Justice," 12.
66. Brown, personal interview, November 10, 2016.
67. Brown, personal interview, November 10, 2016.
68. Brown, personal interview, November 10, 2016.
69. Brown, personal interview, November 10, 2016.
70. Brown, personal interview, November 10, 2016.

Holy Spirit was more real than he had experienced it ever before, the very presence of God "was a welcoming spirit . . . physically."[71] Henri Brown was given unnatural strength during times of difficulty. He noted, "It was somebody else choosing to step in and be the person that was being relied on. I wasn't the person that provided the strength or the words in that moment. I wasn't the one who was doing that."[72] Henri Brown recalled that during his period of struggle, he was upheld by "God acting through me . . . he decided to sustain me with the burdens I couldn't take on myself. When I needed him the most."[73]

Henri described his experience of being carried by God as if it were an athletic event that a person trains for, like a swim meet. Henri explained,

> For swimming you swim miles and miles and miles in this pool and you are achy and sore and tired and you can barely walk and you are throwing up on the pool deck cause you are so dehydrated. At swim meets, you swim as fast as you can and you don't get your best time. Every once in a golden while you get up and you think, God, I have been [in second [place] for so long. And this is going to be the worst day in the world. And you dive in and all of a sudden the race is finished and you have your best time and you have no memory of what just happened.[74]

In this swimming metaphor Henri suggested that the Holy Spirit lifts and carries a person through difficult times: "Something kick[s] in and [takes] over. And it is that kind of a feeling of: you know you did it, but you weren't the one who was doing it."[75] Peterson connects the spiritual life like the life cycles of the Negev desert, often stricken by drought, when suddenly there is life-giving rain. He notes, "Our lives are like that—drought-stricken—and

71. Brown, personal interview, November 10, 2016.
72. Brown, personal interview, November 10, 2016.
73. Brown, personal interview, November 10, 2016.
74. Brown, personal interview, November 10, 2016.
75. Brown, personal interview, November 10, 2016.

then, suddenly, the long years of barren waiting are interrupted by God's invasion of grace.[76]

Henri Brown explained that during periods of extremely exhausting suffering God was with him. He explained, "I have felt his presence every day because that was the only way I woke back up from what was going on in my own life. Just the things I had seen and things I had experienced and I was totally unprepared for and I still came out being myself and not having any kind of lasting repercussion."[77] In Deuteronomy 1:31, Moses recalled God's role in the life of Israel, and his guidance he gave the Hebrew people from the Exodus from Egypt and throughout the forty years wandering in the wilderness. Moses uses language to indicate God carrying his people, "The Lord your God, who is going before you, will fight for you, as he did for you in Egypt, before your very eyes, and in the wilderness. There you saw how the Lord your God carried you, as a father carries his son, all the way you went until you reached this place" (Deut 1:31). Again, in Isaiah 40:11, the prophet Isaiah compares God to a shepherd: "He tends his flock like a shepherd: He gathers the lambs in his arms and carries them close to his heart; he gently leads those that have young."

Henri Brown expressed that while he should have been affected deeply from loss in his life, he was held by the Holy Spirit. He described his experience: "I know other people with similar stories at Gonzaga. . . . One guy who committed suicide last year from a situation . . . he had loss in his life. He couldn't take it and committed suicide. . . . I knew him, so yeah, it affected me. But even thinking about that this summer when I was like, well why did his death not affect me as viscerally as it affected others? Because I felt a presence there, I was willing to just let the presence take over."[78]

Henri Brown explained the role of the Holy Spirit in the lives of others, and how he sees God in other people, "In these moments of just such raw emotion and raw exposure to what is in people's

---

76. Peterson, *Long Obedience*, 100.
77. Brown, personal interview, November 10, 2016.
78. Brown, personal interview, November 10, 2016.

hearts. That is . . . the Holy Spirit that comes in and indwells a person. There is the proof right there when you see what is in someone's heart when they are pushed to their breaking point."[79] Henri noted that the Holy Spirit is at work in his life, and in the lives of those around him. "If asked to define Ignatian spirituality, the first thing out of their mouths would most likely be finding God in all things."[80]

In explaining his capacity to teach in an area outside of his expertise, Henri Brown connected his ability to the work of the Holy Spirit. Although "the first couple of months were bumpy," Henri explained that his ability to teach outside of his ability "is the spirit's work right there."[81] April Garcia illustrated the importance of the role of the Holy Spirit in leading spiritual conversations: "So I think it is just a collection of those moments where I know that is not just me who am acting there. That is me leaning on a different understanding that is greater than my own. And also having them mutually love and support me at the same time to get them to a place where they feel good and I feel good too because I know I'm comforted in knowing that we are both kind of on this spiritual journey together."[82] Martin Buber suggested that God is everywhere. He contended, "In truth, there is no God-seeking because there is nothing where one could not find him."[83] As suggested by Henri, Lloyd, and April, it is possible to see the work of God in all of life's intricacies.

Lloyd White shared about a time in his life that brought deep sadness. He noted that hearing about devastating news from home "totally threw me off," raising questions and "a lot of whys and wrestling and just confusion."[84] He observed that some of life's struggles have become "a new reality."[85] Lloyd White noted that

79. Brown, personal interview, November 10, 2016.
80. Martin, *Jesuit Guide*, 2.
81. Brown, personal interview, November 10, 2016.
82. Garcia, focus group interview, November 4, 2016.
83. Buber, *I and Thou*, 128.
84. White, personal interview, November 13, 2016.
85. White, personal interview, November 10, 2016.

whenever he has been faced with a difficult time in his life, he has had spiritual support. "It is weird how there was always this support system somehow put in place right before a low. . . . I believe that there is somebody upstairs looking down on me and looking out for me."[86] Lloyd was quick to connect the role of relational support with God's goodness and grace in his life.

Megan Pile observed that becoming a person of faith has not helped her feel better in life, nor happier, yet somehow she has been changed by her faith. She explained, "I feel like since I have started my spiritual journey, the world is pooping on me all the time."[87] Yet in the places of despair, "probably one of the darkest semesters I have ever experienced," Megan remembered the gift of people who encouraged her. During her Thursday evenings serving at the House of Charity, a homeless shelter in Spokane, "God just placing these people in my life who would recognize me and thank me or just praise God in all of this."[88] Leaving each evening after serving, Megan always felt "there is a God and we are all so much more connected."[89] She relayed, "I don't think I would be as deeply spiritual as I am today if it wasn't for the darkness. I don't think I would be the leader I am today if it wasn't for the darkness."[90] Megan noted the connection between her growth as a human being and as a leader to going through difficult periods, working through them, and coming out stronger on the other side.

Continuing the discussion on growth and darkness, Jill Kind noted, "I feel like my darkest moments are when I feel guilty or shameful . . . but then from that is always growth."[91] In the darker moments of life, Jill would continue to go "through processes of . . . pushing God away and saying I got this. Whether it is being cocky or . . . [feeling] like I'm not deserving of love."[92] Yet, in the midst of

86. White, personal interview, November 10, 2016.
87. Pile, focus group interview, November 3, 2016.
88. Pile, focus group interview, November 3, 2016.
89. Pile, focus group interview, November 3, 2016.
90. Pile, focus group interview, November 3, 2016.
91. Kind, focus group interview, November 3, 2016.
92. Kind, focus group interview, November 3, 2016.

struggling to carry her own burden, God is present, and the Holy Spirit is at work. Caleb Williams shared the role of the Holy Spirit while working at a Christian camp, "I came at each day with . . . a renewed energy and strength that—that wasn't me. That is God. . . . That connection is what . . . drives me in spirituality I guess. Building that relationship [with God] because it fulfills me and brings me purpose and joy to things I don't think I could have."[93]

To describe the work of God in their lives, many of the students used metaphor, explaining the times where God carried them, or served them in the midst of their suffering and pain. Henri Brown and Liam Black both referred to the work of God in their lives as a carrying of their burden, a sustaining of their bodies and minds. Henri and Liam both mentioned the poem footprints in the sand, recalling periods in their lives that they were carried by God. Liam explained the poem that Jesus is "walking next to you when you are going through life, but when you are really struggling he is carrying you."[94] Henri explained how the story connected with his experience at Gonzaga for the past two years, "I can honestly say I have been carried cause there is no way that I could have done anything. . . . Cause it wasn't me doing it. . . . That is how I have seen change and how God has come in."[95]

Liam Black likewise noted the involvement of God in sustaining him. He related Jesus to "a parent who sees you go through life that they are just there for you. You can have as much conversation with them or as little . . . but it is Jesus walking with you."[96] The sustaining work of the Holy Spirit in the lives of students can explain how and why students were comforted during periods of deep suffering, and often felt that the suffering promoted their growth and reliance upon God.

Sara Green recalled a time leading a Search retreat with the University Ministry department, noting that her role on Search as a servant is similar to God's role in her life. She explained that

93. Williams, focus group interview, November 4, 2016.
94. Black, personal interview, November 13, 2016.
95. Brown, personal interview, November 10, 2016.
96. Black, personal interview, November 13, 2016.

although the students participating on the retreat were unaware, there was a back crew continually working for them and praying for their experience: "You are going to go through these moments where you think no one else is there and you feel completely alone. You are also confused. But then God does show up. . . . He was there all along, he was working on something else and he was waiting for the right time. It was just like wow, even at my lowest of lows, it doesn't mean God is gone. It means God is working on something to deliver at the moment I need it. So that was a profound experience and it kept my faith on this high."[97] To Sara, the profound metaphor of God working in the background, being present in the midst of suffering, provided her a new way to process her suffering.

---

97. Green, personal interview, November 11, 2016.

7

The Path toward Spiritual Resilience

RESILIENT LEADERS ARE ABLE to face increasingly difficult challenges by developing healthy life rhythms and by taking time for reflection. Mature leaders look to develop spiritual resilience through knowing their story, in asking for help, and by practicing self-care.

Often the practice of reflection and the tension of grappling with faith issues and values can be unsettling. Yet Batson, Schoenrad, and Ventis asserted that the very process of searching and reflecting on values, faith and spirituality could be integral to the growth and development of undergraduate students.[1] Henri Brown explained that although he often felt "low spiritually in the moment" in retrospect, he now regards the experience as a high moment of spiritual growth.[2] "I have seen how I got changed two years later. I now understand how things have happened and progressed since then. This is kind of like it is a high-end insight but in the moment it was not."[3] Hill and Pargament assessed from

---

1. Batson et al., *Religion and the Individual*.
2. Brown, personal interview, November 10, 2016.
3. Brown, personal interview, November 10, 2016.

their research: "While there can be negative consequences of religious struggle, there is also evidence that such struggles can have positive effects on overall growth, and that a crisis in faith can be both necessary and instrumental in promoting personal growth and maturation."[4] Students that struggled spiritually and were challenged indicated that their spiritual identity grew following periods of retrospective reflection.

The role of reflection provides space for clarity of thought, and peace, alleviating stress and pain. Lloyd White found that only in retrospect and reflection was he able to see the pattern of God's work in his life. He contended that during the interview process when he was asked to write out the highlights and lowlights of his spiritual journey and leadership journey he was able to see something completely new in his life story. He explained this new clarity: "not knowing it until maybe now, looking at this [pattern] and realizing it."[5] Reflection can take place through story-telling, building self-awareness, and insight, and leading to spiritual and leadership health and self-care.

Knowing One's Story

Throughout the process of the interview, students were asked to reflect on their spiritual and leadership history, highlighting low points and high points, and expressing their understanding of what it means to be a leader, a spiritual person, and how they integrate or struggle to integrate their spirituality into their everyday lives. During interviews, student participants engaged with the focus group, and with myself as an interviewer, compiling his or her story of spiritual and leadership experiences with vigor, often creating new meaning in the process of the interview.

The process of storytelling, according to qualitative researchers, provided an opportunity for the students interviewed to create meaning through the act of telling their spiritual stories. Astin

---

4. Hill and Pargament, "Advances in the Conceptualization," 102.
5. White, personal interview, November 13, 2016.

The Path toward Spiritual Resilience

and coauthors found that among college students, "Leadership skills are enhanced by 'inner work,' including meditation and self-reflection. . . . Meditation and self-reflection, of course, can enhance self-awareness . . . faculty use of reflective writing/journaling as a pedagogical tool increases students' self-understanding and understanding of others, both key factors in leadership."[6] Tristan Jones reflected on his experience leading a spiritual group on campus, and related that during the interview he experienced a spiritual moment. He explained, "Thinking back on it, I'm just like oh my gosh. I see God again. Just all these weird steps leading up to at the beginning of the semester. . . . And just God took it over . . . seeing the other freshmen . . . people who [have] helped restart it again."[7]

During the focus group period a student recalled how she had met God during the worship time that Tristan had organized her first year at Gonzaga. Tristan recalled his response to hearing her mention this during the focus group, "I wanted to cry . . . just because if that was all the group was for—was one person encountering God—then that was enough [and] was worth it."[8] Following the focus group, Tristan noted, "I rushed home after and was like guys, guys, guys, [someone] said this. . . . Just humbling and really makes me feel like I was used a bit. . . . It is up there as a huge God moment in my life. . . . And you helped make that connection. Obviously cool things are coming out of this study."[9]

For Sara Green, she was in the midst of struggling with her spirituality and faith during the focus group and interview process. She explained the encouragement she felt in connecting relationally about issues of spirituality during the interview, "I love moments like this as well where we are in this communal space and we are all talking about our faith. We all feel connected because we are all touching right now in this higher, divine, human, authentic entity. I just find that—it lights me up. It makes me so happy and

6. Astin et al., *Cultivating the Spirit*, 132.
7. Jones, personal interview, November 11, 2016.
8. Jones, personal interview, November 11, 2016.
9. Jones, personal interview, November 11, 2016.

it makes me feel fully human. It is like as if it affirms the purpose we all have here."[10] The very process of constructing information during the interview did have an impact on the continued spiritual growth and formation of participants.

Asking for Help

Following periods of suffering and loss, individuals have the potential to lead with great insight, yet without reflection an experience can just be merely painful and not helpful to oneself or others. In *Teaching a Stone to Talk*, poet Annie Dillard writes,

> In the deeps are the violence and terror of which psychology has warned us. But if you ride these monsters down, if you drop with them farther over the world's rim, you find what our sciences cannot locate or name, the substrate, the ocean or matrix or ether which buoys the rest, which gives goodness its power for good, and evil its power for evil, the unified field: our complex and inexplicable caring for each other, and for our life together here. This is given. It is not learned.[11]

Remarkably, many student participants who had experienced deep pain and isolation recognized their spiritual need and reached out to adults and religious mentors to ask for help. This demonstrates vulnerability in authentic leader behavior from the students and what Annie Dillard noted above as "complex and inexplicable caring for each other."[12]

Time, reflection, and self-awareness played a key part in the ability of participants to seek self-care and to ask for help. Student leaders in the study shared that in their struggles and periods of suffering, they did not always respond as they would have liked to spiritually, with great inner fortitude and confidence in God. April Garcia recalled a personal crisis she experienced while in

---

10. Green, focus group interview, November 4, 2016.
11. Dillard, *Teaching a Stone to Talk*, 85.
12. Dillard, *Teaching a Stone to Talk*, 85.

high school, noting, "I just didn't have that resilience to pick myself back up and say ok what failed here and how can I make it better tomorrow. . . . I just kind of let it consume me, rather than think about God in the picture."[13] Following two very difficult years in high school, April questioned and pled with God, "It is no one's fault, but why is God doing this to me? I kind of had this phase of doubt and disbelief. That was the first time I started questioning, well why am I not believing in God and why do I even believe in him in the first place? Why do I only think these things after [a difficult period]? . . . I just felt so far from my faith. It was just like it was so numb to me."[14]

In retrospect, April Garcia recognized that her spirituality informs her whole life, even in the midst of struggles. April noticed from her senior year of high school, "The times I struggle[d] the most was when I was going through a lot of extra stuff outside of that leadership classroom. With that extra stuff came a lack of spirituality in that I think that when I wasn't feeling close to God, I wasn't feeling close to myself even. I really didn't have that self-awareness."[15] Although in high school, April did not feel she could respond to her suffering, in college, she adapted and changed her approach. She recalled, "I was struggling a lot this last weekend, coming to terms of feeling kind of spiritually empty and feeling just a lot of weird emotions from the summer."[16] While in the midst of spiritual crisis, April Garcia asserted that usually, "I just don't have the energy to look for [God] in my life when I'm going through bad things."[17] Yet, in this moment, April recognized her need for help, and began to seek spiritual direction. She explained, "I just need help. So I went, I sat down, I told her everything going on."[18] A key part in staying spiritually healthy for students included spiritual practices and self-care.

13. Garcia, personal interview, November 12, 2016.
14. Garcia, personal interview, November 12, 2016.
15. Garcia, personal interview, November 12, 2016.
16. Garcia, personal interview, November 12, 2016.
17. Garcia, personal interview, November 12, 2016.
18. Garcia, personal interview, November 12, 2016.

Practicing Self-Care

In integrating faith and spiritual life with everyday action, participants explained the many practices and actions of faith integration. Sharon Parks notes, "Faith arises from the hunger for authenticity, for correspondence between one's inner and outer lives."[19] Tristan Jones contended that in his faith life he has sought to connect with God in authentic ways, "[I] made it more personal, made it really show that relationship with Jesus and the love you can see. . . . Definitely being more intentional with Scripture [and prayer]. Kind of taking doing things on my own more, [and] not [only] in these formal [settings]."[20] Tristan continued, explaining that although difficult to incorporate spiritual practices and self-care, "it is choosing to be intentional with my free time that I do have throughout a busy week. To sit down, read, even just listen to some music."[21]

In the study, some participants discussed the importance of building up a strong and resilient faith and spiritual life through spiritual practices of self-care. Palmer notes, self-care "is never a selfish act—it is simply good stewardship of the only gift I have, the gift I was put on earth to offer to others. Anytime we can listen to true self and give it the care it requires, we do so not only for ourselves but for the many others whose lives we touch."[22] Liam Black described the need for building an intentional relationship with God. He explained, "I need to be focused through having a relationship with God to not be on the autopilot. To make more effective decisions for myself."[23]

Following a difficult time abroad where she was unable to practice her faith fully, Jessie Gray realized "I just need to take care of myself differently . . . the way I was doing that was not good."[24]

19. Parks, *Big Questions, Worthy Dreams*, 16.
20. Jones, personal interview, November 11, 2016.
21. Jones, personal interview, November 11, 2016.
22. Palmer, *Let Your Life Speak*, 30–31.
23. Black, personal interview, November 13, 2016.
24. Gray, personal interview, November 12, 2016.

She spent time considering how to incorporate spiritual practices back into her life and "go back to some of the things I like doing."[25] She noted the many ways spirituality affects her actions. She explained, "My spirituality for me personally is part of the reason I'm a vegetarian. [And] my faith is part of the reason why I go to church on Sunday."[26] Jessie Gray enjoyed spiritual practices like yoga that allowed her "to be outside of myself, outside of the present, like a retreat. It is like a little 40-minute retreat from your life. I think that is just a really important recharging time for me. It is an important time to just really be there . . . sometimes it is prayerful; sometimes it is no thoughts at all. It depends on what I feel like I need that day. But it is just something that I think has become really important to me."[27]

Jessie Gray recognized that spiritually, "to be an effective friend, to be any of that I need to take care of myself and I'm not always very good at that."[28] Yet interestingly, Jessie has found resistance to her personal self-care from peers: "Just because other people don't value them or other people are like well you got to study. Are you sure you should be going to yoga. . . . Because people think they know how I should live my life."[29]

Joy Smith reasoned that busyness could often affect her spirituality, faith, and effectiveness as a relational leader, "A lot of times it is the beginning of semester community is really strong for me because I have more time and I like always am starting new. So I'm going to give myself this period of time every single day to be just focusing on my faith. Then as the semester goes on . . . I'm just bogged down with school and I don't feel like my spirituality is as strong."[30] To remain resilient and effective as a student and a leader, spiritual disciplines such as rest and solitude should be incorporated into weekly rhythms.

25. Gray, personal interview, November 12, 2016.
26. Gray, personal interview, November 12, 2016.
27. Gray, personal interview, November 12, 2016.
28. Gray, personal interview, November 12, 2016.
29. Gray, personal interview, November 12, 2016.
30. Smith, focus group interview, November 3, 2016.

Unscripted Spirituality

American Catholic writer and mystic Thomas Merton persuaded that work must naturally couple with rest if people are to fully embody the kingdom of God: "There is a pervasive form of contemporary violence... [and that is] activism and overwork.... To allow oneself to be carried away by a multitude of conflicting concerns, to surrender to too many demands, to commit oneself to too many projects, to want to help everyone in everything, is to succumb to violence."[31] Like Merton's assertion that workaholic tendencies destroy personal peace, Edwards asserted that the Judeo-Christian spiritual tradition of Sabbath could provide the observer with the peace lacking in her/his inner life. "An understanding and living of Sabbath time can help support a sane and holy rhythm of life for us. With it, we are given an alternative to the culture's growing movement between driven achievement and narrow escape time."[32]

Although seemingly illogical, the spiritual practice of solitude can also develop within an individual a greater sense of community. Merton, Catholic priest and author, mentioned: "It is in deep solitude that I find the gentleness with which I can truly love my brothers. The more solitary I am, the more affection I have for them. It is pure affection and filled with reverence for the solitude of others."[33] Joy noted her ability to enter into community is tied to times of solitude. She explained, "I do feel like the less confident in my leadership, my abilities or what I'm doing, I think it is the times when I'm not giving myself that time alone. That time alone will allow me to then take it out into relationships."[34] Nouwen, an author, Catholic priest and educator, spoke about solitude: "In solitude we can pay attention to our inner self.... In solitude we can become present to ourselves.... There we also can become present to others by reaching out to them, not greedy for attention and affection but offering our own selves to help build a community of love."[35]

31. Merton, *Conjectures of a Guilty Bystander*, 73.
32. Edwards, *Sabbath Time*, 18.
33. Merton, *Sign of Jonas*, 261.
34. Smith, focus group interview, November 3, 2016.
35. Nouwen, *Reaching Out*, 42.

The Path toward Spiritual Resilience

In allowing herself room to care for herself spiritually, Joy Smith noted, "I forget that it is ok to take time away from those things to do something totally unrelated that is only directed at my faith. To get reconnected."[36] Spiritual practices of self-care, including solitude and rest, have the ability to create space for depth of reflection, making sense of periods of stress and suffering. Interestingly, during the focus groups and individual interview process, student participants mentioned that the very act of being interviewed and reflecting on their spiritual journeys, helped in their spiritual self-care.

---

36. Smith, focus group interview, November 3, 2016.

8

The Emergence of Spiritual and Leadership Congruence

INTEGRATING SPIRITUALITY AND LEADERSHIP into actions and practices can be a difficult task for undergraduate students to process and explore. Some of the student participants found the language around spiritual leadership intimidating, or found moments of theological tension. However, many acknowledged the importance of building relationships with those they led, and the natural connection between their personal leadership practices and spirituality and faith beliefs. One such area of spiritual integration was in the way students looked to provide comfort in the same way that they received comfort from the Holy Spirit of God.

An area of theological tension for students in faith and spiritual integration was when they came up against a prescribed truth, passed down from parents, or the church. In determining spiritual and faith identity, students explained the challenge of balancing traditional Catholic and Protestant faith values and expectations along with their personal beliefs around key issues of today.

Issues of abortion and sexual identity are important to students, and as they balance their beliefs with the teaching of the church and parents, they can face a crisis of faith and identity. Sara

The Emergence of Spiritual and Leadership Congruence

Green explained, "Whether or not I am maybe not supportive but I'm with someone who is getting an abortion—does that mean I'm less Catholic? Whether or not you know I'm attending a wedding for two male friends who are getting married, does that mean I'm less Catholic? I don't know. I'm figuring that out."[1]

Her first year of college, Sara encountered a friend sobbing in the basement who discovered she was pregnant. "You know when I was with her I was thinking, I have a couple hundred dollars in my bank account. I will help you. You have a couple of friends—we are going to help you. Whatever you end up doing, we will help you. I'm not saying you should get an abortion, but I am saying whatever you believe to be right, I'm going to be with you. If you are afraid to go alone, I will go with you."[2] In seeking to support a friend who was considering having an abortion, Sara Green recalled her mixed feelings following her conversation, "So then that night I was like oh my God, I'm a horrible Catholic. Oh my God. Oh my God. I'm doing such a wrong thing. God is probably mad at me. So, then I went to [a] Father [on campus] and I told him—this is what I told this girl and this is what I still believe in my core—is that wrong? Am I wrong? Is God mad at me? Did I sin? I don't know."[3]

Sara Green dealt with the tension she was experiencing by seeking help from a Catholic priest, "I explained to him: I have always been taught in a textbook that abortion is wrong. . . . My dad has always pounded it into my head that it is wrong and you can't even think about it. Don't even consider that side for a second . . . but I had never personally encountered that."[4] Exposed to complex real life situations, Sara faced a dilemma, and an individual who needed her direct help. So, in supporting her friend considering an abortion, which goes against the teaching of the Catholic faith, Sara was torn, and questioning the value of her spiritual identity.

---

1. Green, personal interview, November 11, 2016.
2. Green, personal interview, November 11, 2016.
3. Green, personal interview, November 11, 2016.
4. Green, personal interview, November 11, 2016.

Unscripted Spirituality

She had to weigh the imperative to help those in need, and also to potentially disagree with the practice of abortion.

Tristan Jones also connected a feeling of dissonance in integrating his former values with his new faith once he decided to become a follower of Christ: "I felt strongly about gay marriage and marriage equality. I was like, do I need to go back and rethink this sort of thing? I have my faith now. I had that as a value in my life, very much from my family. I was like are these not compatible any longer?"[5] For students caught in the middle of personal belief and church values and theology, they moved toward questioning their very spiritual identity. There is often a stereotype of postmodern millennial Christians as individuals who choose cultural values that are easy over the pursuit of spiritual "truth." This was not the case with the participants I interviewed. They grappled deeply with cultural and theological issues, and sought to balance their faith and beliefs with the doctrine of the church. Integrating spirituality and religious values into the lives of the Christian church is not unique to emerging adults, but is a constant struggle for many Christians.

In considering how to live out their spirituality, student leaders look for places of congruence between belief and action. Sara Green explained her process of figuring out what it means to be Catholic, "I guess being a Catholic is not something you are. It is something that you are actively participating with. . . . I think my faith is more interactive. It is not 'I have to know every single thing about what it means to be Catholic.' Maybe it is just that it is a relationship that I have to care and nurture for. Within that, I will figure out what these beliefs are."[6] As student leaders make meaning of their spiritual lives, they are faced with questions about how to incorporate their faith with their leadership, and their leadership identity.

Lloyd White noted the importance of connecting his faith to his leadership "is not as much transactional as relational and kind of a building up [and] coaching. . . . It is just more real. It is not as

---

5. Jones, personal interview, November 11, 2016.
6. Green, personal interview, November 11, 2016.

superficial. There is depth."[7] He recalled how older peers modeled a style of spiritual leadership he now attempts to emulate, "Seeing how they carried themselves I think with people and faith and how they just intertwined it all was really inspiring. It was a next level of leadership that I noticed. Because it began to make that connection through spirituality so much stronger than it is when it is not there."[8] Joy Smith noted that in choosing to lead, foremost, she strives toward love, "because of certain gifts I have been given, maybe of those relational aspects or the gift of wanting to lead and wanting to be on the forefront of something."[9] Joy mentioned that she connects her faith to her actions, "Through what I choose to do. So, whether that is [having] an internship that I really love and [desire for] my career path . . . I do think [that] adds to my spiritual wellbeing, if I love what I'm doing."[10]

Connecting her leadership, spirituality and faith, Jessie Gray noted, "I think that to know and understand and love others, I must understand that [spiritual] aspect of them."[11] Sara Green agreed, noting, "I think understanding where someone is spiritually and just how they are doing in general, really affects how we can best be of service to those we want to lead or are trying to lead."[12] April Garcia shared about her spirituality shaped her new concept of leadership, "I recognize all my best moments . . . came from when I felt really spiritual with people, when I felt just really deep connection. And that is kind of what is driving my new leadership theory that I am forming for myself is just this idea of human connection."[13]

Henri Brown explained that in leadership he looks forward not only to giving back, but also, to "show people I am a person

---

7. Green, personal interview, November 11, 2016.
8. White, personal interview, November 13, 2016.
9. Smith, personal interview, November 10, 2016.
10. Smith, personal interview, November 10, 2016.
11. Gray, focus group interview, November 4, 2016.
12. Green, personal interview, November 11, 2016.
13. Garcia, personal interview, November 12, 2016.

Unscripted Spirituality

of faith. I'm here because of my faith and here's why."[14] For Henri Brown, his leadership is clearly connected to authentically practicing his faith and living out his values. He asserted,

> You can't disconnect your experience from your spirituality. That is when it forms who you are and we always talk about this concept of genuine leaders. If you are going to be a genuine leader, you have to put that spirituality out as something that is in the forefront of what you are doing. [It] doesn't have to be the main driving force but it has to be something that characterizes your actions. Otherwise, you are not being genuine with the people you are trying to lead and they are not getting to see a whole picture of you if they are not getting to see this part of your life that has such an important part of forming who you are. . . . Our spirituality has to inform our leadership.[15]

Based on his reading of the catechism and of scripture, Henri exclaimed, "If we are supposed to live our faith right then our faith calls us to change our whole being. To me it is kind of like the next step in the process. . . . If you want to live out your faith and you want to call it spiritual leadership, embracing your spirituality, whatever that is, it is an all-consuming change."[16] Henri Brown continued, "Your argument for how you are going to live your life and how other people should live their lives, essentially as leaders, relies basically on your actions, not on your words."[17]

Spiritual conversations and connections with peers offer students a space to be authentic in expressing themselves and offering spiritual care. April Garcia acknowledged the importance of sharing her faith with her peers: "I realize it is a really spiritual moment for me."[18] April explained that although her leadership position and the beginning of the semester was a "big growth period" for her,

---

14. Brown, personal interview, November 10, 2016.
15. Brown, personal interview, November 10, 2016.
16. Brown, personal interview, November 10, 2016.
17. Brown, personal interview, November 10, 2016.
18. Brown, personal interview, November 10, 2016.

"it was really spiritual too because a lot of the conversations were surrounding my faith and how my faith was going to play out in my role."[19] April noted her leadership and spiritual highlights are: "those moments where someone is really down and I get to help facilitate their dignity and their worth back out of them and help them kind of see it."[20] She recalled a time she was able to positively influence one of her peers going through a difficult period: "She came to my room the other night and she said . . . thanks for what you said at dinner tonight, I had never seen it that way before. I'm seeing her make a positive change with what she is doing."[21] Although some participants were uncertain about how spiritual identity connected with their leadership identity, participants easily connected spirituality and faith with building relationships and the concept of holding people in the midst of suffering.

Relational Spirituality

According to Erik Erikson, the search for intimacy is the main psychosocial crisis of this age. "As young adults emerge from adolescence with a sense of identity, they now face the issue of giving that self away in loving, caring, intimate relationships."[22] They are greatly affected by the relationships they form in college and are influenced in who they are and in who they become. For Erikson, the individual is not merely creating an understanding of self in isolation, but within an "enmeshed net of others."[23]

In describing spirituality, participants used vivid words, analogies, and stories to explain that for them, spirituality is relational. Spirituality is lived in community. Wuthnow described the relational nature of spirituality in the United States: "At its core spirituality consists of all the beliefs and activities by which individuals

19. Brown, personal interview, November 10, 2016.
20. Garcia, focus group interview, November 4, 2016.
21. Garcia, focus group interview, November 4, 2016.
22. Wilhoit and Dettoni, *Nurture That Is Christian*, 98.
23. Erikson, *Identity*, 114.

attempt to relate their lives to God or to a divine being or some other conception of a transcendent reality. In a society as complex as that of the United States, spirituality is expressed in many different ways. But spirituality is not just the creation of individuals; it is shaped by larger social circumstances, and by the beliefs and values present in the wider culture."[24] The larger society impacts and builds upon the spirituality of emerging adults, and for many, spirituality is deeply rooted in interpersonal relationships.

Lloyd White explained, "I look at spirituality, faith . . . as a community process and relationship process."[25] April Garcia noted, "For me, spirituality is all about human interaction."[26] Megan Pile defined spirituality as "a connection to something bigger than you or me," continuing, she explained that for her, spirituality "play[s] out in relationships or giving love to other people."[27] Josh Kern agreed, stating that he likewise sees "spirituality, faith, and all that stuff as a community process and relationship process."[28] Participants were unanimous in their explanation of their faith and spirituality as a relational process.

Tristan Jones stressed the importance of relational faith, "I'm always skeptical of people who say, 'I have a private faith.' . . . Faith is meant to be a communal thing. Church is where two or more are gathered in my name. That is where God will be."[29] Eberhard Arnold, founder of the Bruderhof communities, explained the connection of the Christian faith and need for intentional community: "Life in community is no less than a necessity for us—it is an inescapable 'must' that determines everything we do and think. Yet it is not our good intentions or efforts that have been decisive in our choosing this way of life. Rather, we have been overwhelmed by a certainty—a certainty that has its origin and power in the Source of everything that exists. We acknowledge God as

24. Wuthnow, *After Heaven*, viii.
25. White, focus group interview, November 3, 2016.
26. Garcia, personal interview, November 12, 2016.
27. Pile, focus group interview, November 3, 2016.
28. Kern, focus group interview, November 4, 2016.
29. Jones, personal interview, November 11, 2016.

The Emergence of Spiritual and Leadership Congruence

this Source. We must live in community because all life created by God exists in a communal order and works toward community."[30] Sara Green highlighted that in her relationship with God she appreciates Christian unity and the possibility of relationships across opinions, "I can be with God. He is not up there doing rules and regulations. And I can be with people. I don't have to be like well, we both love God but you voted for this so you are over there. . . . We could forget about the other stuff and just remind ourselves we are both human. So let's just be human together with God."[31]

For the Jesuits, "Others are seen as persons whose similar interview with God also takes place, and that is why it is important to listen attentively and to engage with them in sincere dialogue."[32] Sara Green related that although "just a bunch of individuals and we all have our own different relationships with God. . . . At the end of the day, we are all united in this beautiful faith with him."[33] Sara described spirituality as a way to find unity with her peers. In her imagery, she imaged spirituality as a tree, with God as creator, and humanity as the trunk and branches: "We are all part of this common experience. Those branches and those twigs are really all those separate denominations that we identify with. Maybe even if you don't have one to identify with, we are still all a part of this spirituality."[34]

Sara recalled the profound experiences she had on retreats, "Even though we all had very different social views, we all bonded in Christ. It was like we were all going back to our core and it was like we have stripped away every political view, every social view, right now we are just brothers and sisters in Christ."[35] Yet, Tristan did not assume that building community and spiritual relationships

---

30. Arnold, *Writings*, 153.
31. Green, personal interview, November 11, 2016.
32. Álvarez, "Promotion of Justice," 12.
33. Green, focus group interview, November 4, 2016.
34. Green, focus group interview, November 4, 2016.
35. Green, focus group interview, November 4, 2016.

Unscripted Spirituality

is easy, "I think that is something I am aware that I struggle with . . . I don't know if it is self-discipline."[36]

Students highlighted that through relationships with peers, and mentors, they were able to grow in their faith. Jill Kind shared that relationships influence her faith: "When I feel more spiritually connected, I am willing to connect on a deeper level with the people I have relationships with. I'm willing to continue my spiritual growth and their spiritual growth through our connections."[37] Liam Black noted that through his relationship with his girlfriend, he has grown in his faith. He recalled that his relationship "has brought my faith more alive because . . . everybody struggles with their faith, but we help each other in our faith—individually and together."[38] Josh Kern explained that he lives out and expresses his spirituality in relationships, "I think about the past couple years being in college, it has been through relationships that I think I've grown and struggled the most, in the best way possible. . . . My house has been awesome in this journey with me."[39] Jill Kind asserted that when she is strong spiritually she is able to support and strengthen the faith of others: "It is natural for me to feel comfortable in a place of pushing someone else in their spirituality or faith. . . . In relationships with friends, I will realize all of a sudden that I'm in this really deep conversation."[40]

Tristan Jones explained that "people and community have been a really big part of my spirituality" from the beginning of his faith journey.[41] He began to "realize and explore [his] personal faith" in community when he attended a parachurch camp and youth group.[42] Tristan Jones exclaimed that he has best seen God through his relationships with other people, particularly as an extrovert; "I think there is definitely a spiritual energy, a faith energy

---

36. Jones, personal interview, November 11, 2016.
37. Kind, focus group interview, November 3, 2016.
38. Black, personal interview, November 13, 2016.
39. Kern, focus group interview, November 4, 2016.
40. Kind, focus group interview, November 3, 2016.
41. Jones, focus group interview, November 3, 2016.
42. Jones, focus group interview, November 3, 2016.

The Emergence of Spiritual and Leadership Congruence

that I need" from a faith community.[43] Tristan Jones explained, "I think it is an encouragement. I think it is a motivation too, pretty synonymous.... If people are speaking into where they are seeing God, I think it makes me more conscious of ways I am seeing him. And if ... I'm not, it ... motivates me to ... look more actively and just be more active."[44] He explained that his peers influenced his faith greatly: "You could see that difference and they pointed to Jesus when you asked or even if you didn't, they are pointing you to Jesus."[45]

In the midst of difficult periods of life, Jill Kind commented that relationships are essential to her faith, "that draws me out of it and then just being able to have someone else listen or accept what I'm going through.... Or if I can take a glimpse into what someone else is going through, that is what kind of brings me back out of that and I think reconnects me to God. Helps me talk to him, ask him for strength. So I guess it is like realizing that I am not in it alone. I don't have to be alone.... We are all in this together."[46]

Caleb Williams explained that in his faith "there is this joy, unexplainable joy that you get when something clicks."[47] Caleb continued, "When you have a community that comes together and is on the same page, you ... feel this connection ... to God.... It brought me a ton of joy and life."[48] Participants' emphasis on relational spirituality is likewise seen in their desire to lead through the building of relationships.

Relational Leadership

Participants in the focus group and personal interviews emphasized the importance of building relationships with their peers and

---

43. Jones, focus group interview, November 3, 2016.
44. Jones, focus group interview, November 3, 2016.
45. Jones, personal interview, November 11, 2016.
46. Kind, focus group interview, November 3, 2016.
47. Williams, focus group interview, November 4, 2016.
48. Williams, focus group interview, November 4, 2016.

colleagues in order to be effective leaders. Leadership theorists Allen and Cherrey noted, "Relationships are the connective tissue of the organization . . . over time, these new relationships, built on trust and integrity, become the glue that holds us together."[49] Jessie Gray explained that "knowing people and understanding them" is central in leading at Gonzaga.[50] She asserted that in her new leadership role with interfaith dialogue on campus, "a really big drive for that is that I think that we are called to know and to understand people."[51] Sara Green likewise highlighted that building relationships with her coworkers helped her to be an effective leader, "I think caring for them outside of just being my employee . . . [and] while at work, makes the leadership at work much stronger."[52]

The Relational Leadership Model, largely aspirational, "view[s] leadership as a relational and collaborative process," and emphasizes "being ethical and creating positive change for the greater good."[53] While maintaining different definitions than the Spiritual Formation Model (see figure 2) of cognitive thinking, inward journey and outward expression, the Relational Leadership Model follows three basic principles of knowing, being, and doing. Komives and coauthors suggest leaders must be self-aware, knowing "how change occurs, and how and why others may view things differently," be "ethical, principled, authentic, open, caring and inclusive," and "must act in socially responsible ways, consistently and congruently, as participants in a community," with "commitments and passions."[54] Outcomes associated with socially responsible leadership include positive leadership outcomes from faculty interaction and mentoring, self-awareness and peer interactions across difference.

Student participants in this study did not focus on many of the same elements as Komives and coauthors in their understanding

49. Allen and Cherrey, *Systemic Leadership*, 31.
50. Gray, focus group interview, November 4, 2016.
51. Gray, focus group interview, November 4, 2016.
52. Green, focus group interview, November 4, 2016.
53. Komives, Lucas, and McMahon, *Exploring Leadership*, 460.
54. Komives, Lucas, and McMahon, *Exploring Leadership*, 7.

The Emergence of Spiritual and Leadership Congruence

of relational leadership, yet there are some interesting overlaps. The participants, all students at a Jesuit university, included in this study connected their leadership and service motivation to their practice of relational spirituality, and care for the common good. Álvarez explained the Jesuit approach to serving: "In modern times, democracies require responsible citizens who participate in public affairs, promote equal opportunity, and commit themselves to working together for the common good."[55]

Relational leadership is deeply connected to participants' relational spirituality, the desire to serve God for the common good. Evelyn Underhill wrote about the Christian mystics and the emphasis of charity, or outward service, as a significant part in forming a spiritual life with God. She notes, "The fire of charity, lit in the soul, needs careful tending. The first tiny flame must not be allowed to die down for lack of fuel; and we may have to feed it with things we should prefer to keep for ourselves. It will only be developed and kept burning in a life informed by prayer—faithful, steady, mortified, self-oblivious prayer, the humble aspiration of the spirit to its Source: indeed the very object of prayer is to increase and maintain charity, the loving friendship of the soul with God."[56] She explains, "The cross is the supreme symbol of that double movement of charity; the pouring forth of self-oblivious love, up towards God, outwards towards men, and surely downwards too, to all the smaller children of God."[57] Relational leadership is deeply spiritual and therefore deeply human, connecting an individual with God and all humanity through relationship.

Lloyd White shared that during his work life and leadership roles at Gonzaga he would like to be known as a relational leader, "I think somebody who is willing to go the extra mile for people, to be authentic in relationship, and not somebody who is totally focused on the end goal. . . . Being somebody who cares more about the people and the process rather than the dollar sign at the end."[58]

55. Álvarez, "Promotion of Justice," 9.
56. Underhill, *Essential Writings*, 54.
57. Underhill, *Essential Writings*, 56.
58. White, personal interview, November 13, 2016.

Sara Green felt that as a leader, being in relationship with those in the Gonzaga community was mutually beneficial. She expressed that while engaging "with people at GU" her "leadership was on fire."[59] In relating to people, Sara acknowledged that as a relational leader, she attempts to adapt her approach to meet the needs of each person she leads: "How [a peer] is doing really affects how I approach her and how I can be the best help to her."[60]

Joy Smith suggested that while at Gonzaga she changed the style of leadership she practiced, she no longer just focused on reaching tasks and goals, but realized the importance of building relationships with her colleagues and those she was leading. Joy Smith said, "I have learned that when I get excited about a leadership position, it is not because of the tasks I'm doing. It is because of what I get to do. What impact I get to have. And what that means that I get to be that leader. How I have treated others. It is more like—a relationship with others."[61]

She explained her new approach to connect with her peers and colleagues, "I sit down and I want to know them and want to talk to them because that is the point of it."[62] Joy explained, "Because of those [relational] gifts I'm drawn to love others through my leadership."[63] Joy's expression of love for others is tied into Ignatian spirituality. "For Ignatius, God expresses himself as love, and when he is experienced as such he incites praise and profound sentiments of gratitude in human beings."[64] Joy described how building personal relationships while leading "makes it worth [it] even in the times I'm . . . distant."[65]

April Garcia argued the importance of self-care and passion in developing a style of leadership. She asked, "How can you effectively lead someone else if you don't even really like or desire

59. Green, personal interview, November 11, 2016.
60. Green, personal interview, November 11, 2016.
61. Smith, personal interview, November 10, 2016.
62. Smith, personal interview, November 10, 2016.
63. Smith, personal interview, November 10, 2016.
64. Álvarez, "Promotion of Justice," 12.
65. Smith, personal interview, November 10, 2016.

that thing yourself?"⁶⁶ Joy Smith found that in having passion in leadership, "I can really move people," and in that moment "I really feel like I'm leading because then I'm not just place holding and managing. I'm actually leading a group."⁶⁷ She relates that the "relational piece of the people I get to be with and the people I'm leading," combined with "what I'm doing [and] who that is impacting," continues to motivate her in leadership.⁶⁸ Along with the motivation to be relational, student participants explained their desire to live out their spirituality with empathy, engaging with the concept of holding each other's burdens.

Holding Each Other's Burdens

In connection with suffering and growth, students noted the importance of holding people while leading, and the role that God has played in carrying them through difficult periods. Palmer asserted, "Good leadership comes from people who have penetrated their own inner darkness and arrived at the place where we are one with one another, people who can lead the rest of us to a place of 'hidden wholeness' because they have been there and know the way."⁶⁹ Although most participants often did not consider themselves spiritual leaders on campus, and many openly avoided expressing their faith with their peers, student leaders did engage in spiritual leadership practices, such as coming alongside people in suffering, holding and listening to them, or just being a presence.

In the fall semester of 2016, Gonzaga's University Ministry brought clinical psychologist Dr. Kent Hoffman to campus to speak during a week focused on Suffering and the Soul. The week included activities about issues of suffering, and occurred a few weeks prior to my interviews with student participants, possibly influencing their discussion about how to integrate spirituality

---

66. Garcia, focus group interview, November 4, 2016.
67. Smith, personal interview, November 10, 2016.
68. Smith, personal interview, November 10, 2016.
69. Palmer, *Let Your Life Speak*, 80–81.

Unscripted Spirituality

and leadership. Students throughout the interviews referred to the concept of holding and being held. There was something very practical and applicable that students connected with in the presentation by Dr. Hoffman.

Multiple students in the focus groups and individual interviews referred to the week and events as helping to shape their philosophy of leadership and spirituality, particularly with the concept of holding people. Josh Kern noted, "In my perspective, I would say that leadership for me is to basically hold people. I think God called us to hold people."[70] In his leadership position, Josh said that in meeting with those he supervises, "I don't go at these from a religious or spiritual background. But I think almost everyone that I have, I attempt at holding them in their best moments and their worst moments. I think that is what God called us to do in our relationships with people."[71] Lloyd White mentioned that he has also experienced this concept of being held, "I have been held by God in a variety of different ways."[72]

Joy Smith recalled the words of Dr. Hoffman, noting "holding and resonance" were important for people experiencing suffering.[73] According to the *Gonzaga Bulletin*, a student newspaper, during his talk, Dr. Hoffman discussed presence and resonance as having a direct correlation with decreasing another individual's pain.[74] He explained that in order to increase presence and resonance in the lives of others, students should engage in "close relationships, psychotherapy, and spiritual practices."[75] From her own experience, Megan Pile discerned, "I think my spirituality . . . has allowed me to go to those deeper places and really talk about the root of suffering and how we are supposed to hold all of these things we experience."[76]

70. Kern, focus group interview, November 4, 2016.
71. Kern, focus group interview, November 4, 2016.
72. White, focus group interview, November 3, 2016.
73. Smith, personal interview, November 10, 2016.
74. Jones, "Dr. Hoffman Speaks."
75. Jones, "Dr. Hoffman Speaks."
76. Pile, focus group interview, November 3, 2016.

The Emergence of Spiritual and Leadership Congruence

Bowlby, a psychologist, first wrote about attachment theory as an ecological and evolutionary approach to understand a child's attachment to his or her mother.[77] Attachment theory suggests that among emerging adults, the period of transition between availability to parental figures and attachment with a romantic partner can create periods of sadness and distress.[78] The concept of holding people connects with attachment theory, as it is strongly relational, encompassing the notion of walking alongside people during their suffering and joyful moments.

Joy Smith noted that her leadership is connected with spirituality through holding people. She explained, "I have been able to lead out of my spirituality. I think it started with me feeling that this is how I can spiritually be with them. . . . I was able to be there and . . . hold them and resonate with them."[79] Joy Smith argued that holding and leading people connected deeply to her practice of spirituality: "I was being a little bit of God's holding for them. I felt like I was providing a peace that wouldn't come from just me, it had to have come from [God]. I realized at that moment how much intentionally leading out of my faith and spirituality and my social teachings from my faith—that I am able to lead faithfully and like lead people to a faithful or spiritual solution of their own."[80]

Jessie Gray explained that in leading her peers, connecting relationally was very important and an expression of her faith. She suggested that "whether you are laughing or having a really deep conversation" during good seasons of life, or whether during a time of suffering, "being held or holding someone in their sorrow and a really low moment. Anything like that is just so God to me."[81] She continued, "Spirituality is all about relationships and holding people and being held and also walking with people."[82]

---

77. Bowlby, "The Nature of the Child's Tie to His Mother."
78. Cassidy and Shaver, *Handbook of Attachment*, 36.
79. Smith, personal interview, November 10, 2016.
80. Smith, personal interview, November 10, 2016.
81. Gray, focus group interview, November 4, 2016.
82. Gray, focus group interview, November 4, 2016.

Unscripted Spirituality

April Garcia likewise contended, "On a greater scale of seeing that spirituality in leadership, I think that a lot of my leadership roles have included me meeting people where they are at, and having . . . a really positive time with them."[83] April noted that she did not have to share openly about her faith with peers or people in order to be spiritual with them. "A lot of times that comes from sharing joy and sharing laughter and just feeling comforted and held in that moment with those people."[84]

Joy Smith explained that she is still trying out the concept of holding in enacting her spirituality and faith: "This is a new concept [for me]. . . . I just learned about it this year so I'm still figuring out what that looks like for me."[85] She found that in practicing holding with peers she was leading, "all of a sudden I felt this really strong sense of awareness of their pain and suffering and just wanted to hold. As I was doing that, I felt that peace."[86] Using her senses, Joy explained what holding felt and looked like for her, "It was more like a sigh for me. . . . I was able to be there and it felt like deep breaths. I felt like that was allowing them to take a deep breath."[87] She continued, "It didn't take away the sadness at all . . . but it just let them be held and let them know they can be sad and it is going to be ok to be sad at least."[88] The integration of spirituality in leading was a natural way for Joy to engage with God, and to provide for others what God had provided for her.

---

83. Garcia, focus group interview, November 4, 2016.
84. Garcia, focus group interview, November 4, 2016.
85. Smith, personal interview, November 10, 2016.
86. Smith, personal interview, November 10, 2016.
87. Smith, personal interview, November 10, 2016.
88. Smith, personal interview, November 10, 2016.

9

Conclusion

Supporting Emerging Adults in College

LIBERAL ARTS UNIVERSITIES HAVE a significant role to play in the development of students as whole persons who can reflect on their values, make meaning of their lives, and serve their communities. "College is an intellectual journey, but it is also a time of inward spiritual journey in which students expect a personal transformation into something new and more complete. If we miss this about students (and we often do), we fail to understand what truly matters most to them."[1] Not only does spirituality matter to emerging adults, but spiritually focused educational practices can also create opportunities for leadership and spiritual identity development, along with integrative and holistic learning. The implications of this study suggest that universities can and should provide support for leadership and spiritual identity development among emerging adults, along with relational support, and support during periods of spiritual crisis and transition.

Developmentally, emerging adults are beginning to discover their voice, their unique talents and their place in the global society. Today's educators are able to facilitate transformative educational

---

1. Chickering et al., *Encouraging Authenticity*, 154.

experiences based on the developmental needs of emerging adults and the environmental conditions helpful to their learning, providing a suitable balance of both challenge and support. In terms of leadership and spiritual identity development, the approach to student learning is key as educators "will be more effective if they approach their work from an end-user's perspective."[2] In this book, I addressed my guiding research questions to such end users, the students themselves, asking: (1) What are students' spiritual experiences during college? (2) How do student leaders make meaning in their lives from spiritual experiences? And, (3) What impact do spiritual experiences have, if any, on students' leadership identity?

To develop greater leadership identity support in a university setting, the findings of this study imply that students require specific leadership training and a campus wide understanding of leadership, or a common language among student leaders. Throughout the study, it became apparent that many of the student leaders were developmentally in the earlier stages of the Leadership Identity Development (LID) model. Komives and coauthors suggest that in stage four of the LID model, a stage wherein many student leaders were developmentally located, educators could "teach communication skills such as active listening and empathy, and identifying the commonality of purpose with other groups."[3] For these particular student participants who already highly value relationship and lean toward empathy, I would suggest student leaders remain in leadership positions for longer than a year, moving toward roles where they are able to train other student leaders, creating opportunities to sustain organizations and think of future plans. A handful of student leaders had already been in positions longer than one year, but none mentioned sustaining the organization or passing along leadership insights to new leaders.

As students transition between leadership identity stages, there is also need for a common language for leadership. In the LID model, "The key transition from stage three to four is facilitated by teaching the language of leadership, helping students

2. Clydesdale, *First Year Out*, 203.
3. Komives et al., "Leadership Identity Model," 416.

learn the contributions others make to group process and to value diverse styles and ideas, and encouraging students to reflect on what they used to think leadership was (object) and what it is to them now (subject)."[4] At Gonzaga, the leadership courses did help students articulate leadership concepts and personal values to a greater extent than those student leaders who did not take the courses or training.

Along with the inclusion of a common language of leadership, one implication of the study is to build a common language around spirituality on university campuses, intentionally addressing how students can integrate spirituality with leadership. To create a common language of spirituality, universities can train faculty and staff to address issues of spirituality in a broad sense through reflective activities, meaning making, and by addressing bigger questions and issues of identity and self-awareness in the classroom and in cocurricular leadership and spiritual training. A posture of authenticity and vulnerability would be particularly helpful for emerging adults.

In terms of spiritual integration, many students struggled to articulate or process how they integrated their spirituality with their lives. Clydesdale noted that "from the perspective of historic religious traditions, [emerging adults today] are quite inarticulate."[5] Providing students with the language and tools to discuss spiritual leadership, and how to integrate personal values with actions, will be helpful, as evidenced in the ability of students who received intensive leadership training in the Comprehensive Leadership Program (CLP) versus students who did not. To help in the process of creating a common language of spirituality, the university can use the spiritual formation model (see figure 2) as a teaching framework, to assist faculty and staff in addressing all areas of spiritual development and formation, including the cognitive thinking, the internal journey and outward service to the broader community.

4. Komives et al., "Leadership Identity Model," 416.
5. Clydesdale, *First Year Out*, 61.

Unscripted Spirituality

The inclusion of spiritual discussion during leadership courses and cocurricular trainings would be helpful in creating a common language. To create spaces of authentic leadership for students, "our public and private selves have to come closer together."[6] Integrative holistic and reflective practices can also be included in the core curriculum, or first year student courses, and at the close of the senior year for comparative reflection experiences. "For the spiritual simply is our life, no matter what grand theories we may hold."[7] Yet, as universities plan and prepare for a spiritual curriculum for students, there must also be awareness that spirituality or religious thought cannot be forced by willpower alone. Willard discusses the growth of the spiritual life as a "renovation of the heart" toward "Christlikeness," not affected by willpower, but "rather . . . all other essential aspects of the person come into line with the intent of a will brought to newness of life 'from above' by the Word and the Spirit."[8] Creating a spiritual dialogue at the university level can be highly influential to enable students to process difficult situations, and to create spaces for students to integrate spirituality with leadership style and practice.

Bringing in scholars and experts to further expand language and give voice to experiences has proven to be helpful, such as the example of Dr. Kent Hoffman visiting campus during the Suffering and the Soul week. Student participants responded very positively to the campus-wide discussion, and found language during that week to inform their spiritual identity. It would be helpful for the campus to provide additional weeks that focus on authentic and holistic topics that allow for and model vulnerability. Palmer wrote that humans naturally long for authenticity in their spiritual lives, a congruence between one's inner and outer life.[9] It may also be helpful for the university to address integrative topics, helping students articulate congruence of faith and lived out experience. The inclusion of spiritual discussion during University Ministry

6. Komives, "Spirituality and Leadership," 12.
7. Willard, *Renovation of the Heart*, 18.
8. Willard, *Renovation of the Heart*, 18, 253.
9. Palmer, "Evoking the Spirit in Public Education."

Conclusion

(UMIN) training and retreats has also proven helpful for student participants, not only creating a space for reflection, but also in creating a spiritual community of belonging.

Although many participants practiced combining spirituality with their leadership styles, some student leaders were unable to clearly articulate their spiritual connection with their leadership roles. Chickering and coauthors found that "striving for integrity—for a life where word and deed, word and word, deed and deed are consistent with a personally owned value structure, over time and across varied contexts—is critical for spiritual integrity and growth."[10] The most prevalent way of describing how student leaders practiced spirituality was connected to building relationships with peers. When discussing who "spiritual leaders" on campus were, Catholic students were uncertain if they could be a spiritual leader on campus as a layperson if they were not adequately trained, or in a specific position. In contrast, Protestant student participants were more comfortable with the concept of integrating his or her spirituality into leadership, and all Protestant students noted that they considered themselves to be spiritual leaders on campus.

The exclusion of spiritual discourse can have the unintended goal of teaching students that spirituality is not of importance to the university. For "just as culture is carried by a living tradition, so too is a particular spirituality."[11] The university teaches both by including and excluding content in the classroom and cocurricular. Holistic education integrates spiritual and leadership discourse. As universities, "we need to create environments that value the integrity of congruence."[12] In light of this information, I suggest that leadership faculty and cocurricular staff look for ways to integrate spirituality in courses and experiential learning opportunities. A posture of authenticity and vulnerability would be particularly helpful for emerging adults.

---

10. Chickering et al., *Encouraging Authenticity*, 9.
11. Barry and Doherty, *Contemplatives in Action*, 2.
12. Komives, "Spirituality and Leadership," 12.

Students are on a journey of spiritual discovery, and important in students' development is the role of a mentor or spiritual guide, whether faculty, parent, peer, staff member, or religious figure. I suggest that through spiritual conversation and an open approach, adult figures are able to help emerging adults process faith ownership and make meaning of difficult life challenges. In this spiritual discovery phase, student participants particularly mentioned interacting with individuals with different faith practices, such as the Evangelical tradition for Catholic students, as a point of faith struggle as well as faith ownership. In light of spiritual ownership and exploration, I suggest that the university create a space for interfaith dialogue on campus, particularly ecumenical conversation between Catholic and Protestant students, or between students of similar faith backgrounds but who have different faith practices.

Along with the university setting, students can also find spiritual and leadership identity support in the home, and in parachurch and religious institutions, such as the local church or a youth group. According to Chickering and coauthors, "The spiritual journey almost always involves traveling companions. An important aspect of the spiritual quest in youth is the desire to connect with others in a deeper and more meaningful way. The tribe is especially important for students because college is typically a place and time of great personal challenge and transition."[13] Student leaders noted the existence of spiritual mentors, but none mentioned the significance of leadership mentors in helping to develop their leadership identity. Higher education is poised to walk with students through existential questions and to provide mentoring and training for leadership as well as for spirituality in their communities.

The role of the mentor and educator is to guide students toward spiritual maturity, and growth for transformation. Greenleaf, an advocate for servant leadership, and longtime advisor to universities of higher education, raised a good point when he asserted that students "may make a quantum leap in their growth

---

13. Chickering et al., *Encouraging Authenticity*, 171.

Conclusion

as responsible persons while they are in college if someone on the faculty takes an interest in finding, and coaching them, much as the athletic department finds and coaches athletes."[14] Reed affirmed the important role of mentors: "Shared experience is educational because a mentor can help guide us to information we might not otherwise use or might use wrongly. Without a mentor we could be wrong and not know why, or we could be right, but still not know why."[15] Spiritual conversations with family, and with older and peer mentors are extremely valuable to emerging adults, particularly in an open and inviting setting where students are allowed to question religious doctrine, and faith tenants, and grapple with questions of how to integrate values and have differences of opinions among peers. Having mentors available to help process differences of religious practices and spiritual questions in an open manner will allow for students to reflect in safety, processing beliefs and how to live out their faith life.

Churches and parachurch ministries also have the opportunity to support college students. According to the Barna Group research, "The current state of ministry to twentysomethings is woefully inadequate to address the spiritual needs of millions of young adults. These individuals are making significant life choices and determining the patterns and preferences of their spiritual reality."[16] In the lives of the participants discussed, churches were noted as an important element of spiritual identity, although not a central part. In the Christian faith, the desert fathers and mothers were the first spiritual directors, offering counsel and advice to those who would travel to the deserts to seek guidance. There is room for further mentorship from religious leaders during the college experience, particularly during periods of transition and questioning. In the study, students indicated self-selecting to ask for help from religious leaders once they had realized a spiritual need for assistance. These particular students felt a level of safety and trust with religious leaders, yet for students who do not, they

---

14. Greenleaf, *Servant as Leader*, 209–10.
15. Reed, *Necessity of Experience*, 114.
16. Kinnaman, "Most Twentysomethings," para 8.

may need religious leaders to reach out to them. The building of relationships with religious leaders can lead to trust and to ongoing spiritual support well after college.

College students face multiple changes during college, including transitions such as study abroad, new leadership positions, or personal or familial challenges. One of the major periods of transition for college students is during their first year of college. That first year, emerging adults may be leaving their family for the first time, and forming their spiritual and leadership identity for the first time. Many universities are focusing on first year student engagement, with the creation of full-time positions to support the first year student experience. At Gonzaga this included a first year student retreat, and a strong emphasis from residence life on helping to create community among first year students. An additional suggestion for cocurricular staff and faculty is to engage students in participation in group settings and entry-level leadership positions during their first year of college. Gaining a leadership position can be very difficult to do with so much competition from upper-class students on campus, and little understanding of campus culture.

College resources of finances, time, and faculty and staff ownership may make any suggestions difficult to enact, so I have included multiple examples of student support during transitions that scale from simple responses, to more engaged. The simplest response is for a discussion with students heading abroad, about the real spiritual and relational challenges they may face, and some individuals they can connect with while abroad, and on campus upon their return. Perhaps students also could be given a reflective assignment to complete before, during and following their abroad experience, such as a reading and a reflective journal with prompts and resources. An example also could include students signing up for a spiritual mentor while living abroad. Students living abroad could receive a phone call from their mentor mid-semester from the university campus staff or faculty, including counselors, university ministry staff, a priest, or a mentor figure. An even more profound connection could include a personal visit from a university spiritual representative, counselor, or mentor. Upon returning to campus, students could attend a specific retreat focusing on periods of transition, or a spiritually meditative service.

Student leaders require a space to process challenges and periods of transition, particularly during the first year of college, and throughout and following periods abroad, and even after the college experience. Reflection, including spiritual discussion with trusted adult figures, can be an excellent tool for processing periods of suffering. In reflection, leaders can potentially shield people from their idiosyncrasies and flaws, and enter into dialogue aware of what Gadamer would describe as their pre-judgments and prejudices.[17] Similar to dealing with leadership struggles and leader flaws, spiritual struggles are not always an easy or pleasant experience.

Although students experiencing religious struggle may indicate a turn away from faith, or have negative consequences for students, religious struggle, like most challenges, can have surprising outcomes. Student participants in this study indicated that spiritual experiences, difficult periods of transition, and challenges led to increased depth of faith and spiritual ownership. According to psychologists, assessing methodology and research in the field of religion and spirituality, spiritual struggle and challenge, such as a crisis of faith, can bring about positive spiritual growth and personal maturity.[18] A crisis of faith, or struggle, should in no way strike panic into the heart of educators, for spiritual struggle, pluralism and openness can be signs of greater tolerance, dialogue and spiritual growth. Trappist monk Thomas Merton wrote, "Our real journey in life is interior; it is a matter of growth, deepening, and of an ever greater surrender to the creative action of love and grace in our hearts."[19]

The experience of learning during transitionary periods and under challenging situations develops growth and creates an opportunity for experiential and holistic education. Palmer asserted

17. Gadamer, *Truth and Method*.
18. Hill and Pargament, "Advances in the Conceptualization."
19. Merton, *Asian Journal*, 296.

that "great leadership comes from people who have made that downward journey through violence and terror, who have touched the deep place where we are in community with each other."[20] To best support these students seeking relationship and a sense of self is to provide opportunities for safe and authentic relationships. It is important to have conversations or teaching centering on how to approach key transitional periods healthily before, during and after transitions.

The university is a unique environment to engage in conversation, dialogue and spiritual and leadership identity development among emerging adults. Chickering and coauthors noted, "To have significant impact, and to ultimately amplify the institutional culture, we need changes that penetrate all aspects of the student experience and that engage all administrators, faculty, student affairs professionals, and staff."[21] An integrated spiritual emphasis at the university level will strengthen student identity development as students deal with transitions, as well as help students become thoughtful, relational leaders who are able to authentically live out their values and beliefs. To best support undergraduate college students, each university must consider how it might unilaterally integrate spirituality, spiritual language, and spiritual practices into its leadership curriculum, strategic planning, and vision.

---

20. Palmer, "Evoking the Spirit," 202.
21. Chickering et al., *Encouraging Authenticity*, 94.

Bibliography

Allen, Kathleen E., and Cynthia Cherrey. *Systemic Leadership: Enriching the Meaning of Our Work*. Washington, DC: National Association of Campus Activities and the American College Personnel Association, 2000.

Álvarez, Paxti. "The Promotion of Justice in the Universities of the Society." *Promotio Iustitiae* 116 (2014). http://www.sjweb.info/documents/sjs/pj/docs_pdf/PJ_116_ENG.pdf.

Amir, Jan. Focus group interview by Luisa J. Gallagher. Spokane, Washington, November 4, 2016. Transcript.

Arnett, Jeffrey J., and Malcolm Hughes. *Adolescence and Emerging Adulthood: A Cultural Approach*. Essex, UK: Pearson Education, 2012.

Arnold, Eberhard. *Eberhard Arnold: Writings Selected*. New York: Plough, 2011.

Arrupe, Pedro. "Men for Others." Address to the Tenth International Congress of Jesuit Alumni of Europe, July 31, 1973, Valencia, Spain. http://onlineministries.creighton.edu/CollaborativeMinistry/men-for-others.html.

Astin, Alexander W., et al. *Cultivating the Spirit: How College Can Enhance Students' Inner Lives*. San Francisco: Jossey-Bass, 2011.

Avolio, Bruce J., and William L. Gardner. "Authentic Leadership Development: Getting to the Root of Positive Forms of Leadership." *Leadership Quarterly* 16 (2005) 315–38.

Bandura, Albert. *Self-Efficacy: The Exercise of Control*. New York: Freeman, 1997.

Barry, William A., and Robert G. Doherty. *Contemplatives in Action: The Jesuit Way*. New York: Paulist, 2002.

Batson, C. Daniel, et al. *Religion and the Individual: A Social Psychological Perspective*. New York: Oxford University Press, 1993.

Baumrind, Diana. "A Developmental Perspective on Adolescent Risk Taking in Contemporary America." *New Directions for Child Development* 37 (1987) 93–125.

Bennis, Warren G. *On Becoming a Leader*. Reading, MA: Addison-Wesley, 1989.

Bibliography

Benson, Peter L., et al. "The Faith Maturity Scale: Conceptualization, Measurement, and Empirical Validation." *Research in the Social Scientific Study of Religion* 5 (1993) 1–26.

Berry, Devon M., and Kate York. "Depression and Religiosity and/or Spirituality in College: A Longitudinal Survey of Students in the USA." *Nursing and Health Sciences* 13 (2011) 76–83.

Black, Liam. Focus group interview by Luisa J. Gallagher. Spokane, Washington, November 4, 2016. Transcript.

———. Personal interview by Luisa J. Gallagher. Spokane, Washington, November 13, 2016. Transcript.

Bowlby, John. "The Nature of the Child's Tie to His Mother." *International Journal of Psycho-Analysis* 39 (1958) 350–73.

Braskamp, Larry A., et al. "Using the Global Perspective Inventory to Assess the Value of Education Abroad." Presentation at the Annual Meeting of Forum on Education Abroad, Charlotte, NC, March 2010.

Brown, Henri. Personal interview by Luisa J. Gallagher. Spokane, Washington, November 10, 2016. Transcript.

Buber, Martin. *I and Thou*. Translated by Walter Kaufmann. New York: Simon and Schuster, 1970.

Burghardt, Walter J. "Contemplation: A Long, Loving Look at the Real." In *An Ignatian Spirituality Reader*, edited by George W. Traub, 89–98. Chicago: Loyola Press, 2008.

Case, Frank E. "Finding God in All Things." *Gonzaga Magazine*, Spring 2012, 47. https://issuu.com/gonzaga/docs/gonzaga-magazine-spring2012-hr.

Cassidy, Jude, and Phillip R. Shaver, eds. *Handbook of Attachment: Theory, Research and Clinical Applications*. New York: Guilford, 1999.

Cherry, Conrad, et al. *Religion on Campus*. Chapel Hill: University of North Carolina Press, 2001.

Chickering, Arthur W., et al. *Encouraging Authenticity and Spirituality in Higher Education*. San Francisco: Jossey-Bass, 2006.

Clydesdale, Tim T. *The First Year Out: Understanding American Teens after High School*. Chicago: University of Chicago Press, 2007.

Collins, W. Andrew, and Brett Laursen. "Parent-Adolescent Relationships and Influences." In *Handbook of Adolescent Psychology*, edited by Richard M. Lerner and Laurence Steinberg, 331–61. Hoboken, NJ: John Wiley, 2004.

Cui, Ming, et al. "Young Adult Romantic Relationships: The Role of Parents' Marital Problems and Relationship Efficacy." *Personality and Social Psychology Bulletin* 34 (2008) 1226–35.

Dean, Jonathan. *A Heart Strangely Warmed: John and Charles Wesley and Their Writings*. Norfolk, UK: Canterbury, 2014.

Dillard, Annie. *Teaching a Stone to Talk: Expeditions and Encounters*. New York: Harper, 2013.

Dugan, John P., and Susan R. Komives. *Developing Leadership Capacity in College Students: Findings from a National Study*. College Park, MD: National Clearinghouse for Leadership Programs, 2007.

Bibliography

Duminuco, Vincent J., ed. *The Jesuit Ratio Studiorum: 400th Anniversary Perspectives*. New York: Fordham University Press, 2000.

Dworkin, Jodi B., and Reed Larson. "Age Trends in the Experience of Family Discord in Single-Mother Families across Adolescence." *Journal of Adolescence* 24 (2001) 529–34.

Edwards, Tilden. *Sabbath Time*. Nashville: Upper Room, 1992.

Erikson, Erik H. *Identity, Youth and Crisis*. New York: Norton, 1968.

Fowler, James W. *Stages of Faith*. New York: HarperCollins, 1981.

Frick, Don. "Understanding Robert K. Greenleaf and Servant-Leadership." Afterword to *Insights on Leadership: Service, Stewardship, Spirit, and Servant-Leadership*, edited by Larry C. Spears, 353–58. Hoboken, NJ: John Wiley, 1998.

Gadamer, Hans-Georg. *Truth and Method*. Translated by Joel Weinsheimer and Donald G. Marshall. New York: Continuum, 1995.

Garcia, April. Focus group interview by Luisa J. Gallagher. Spokane, Washington, November 4, 2016. Transcript.

———. Personal interview by Luisa J. Gallagher. Spokane, Washington, November 12, 2016. Transcript.

Gardner, William L., et al. *Authentic Leadership Theory and Practice: Origins, Effects, and Development*. San Diego: Elsevier, 2005.

Geertz, Clifford. "The Interpretation of Cultures." In *The Interpretation of Cultures: Selected Essays*, 3–30. New York: Basic, 1973.

George, Bill. *Authentic Leadership: Rediscovering the Secrets to Creating Lasting Value*. San Francisco: Jossey-Bass, 2004.

Gonzaga University. "At a Glance: GU Facts and Figures." 2015. http://www.gonzaga.edu/about/ataglance.asp.

———. "Common Data Set 2015–2016: Gonzaga University." 2015. Office of Institutional Research. https://www.gonzaga.edu/campus-resources/offices-and-services-a-Z/office-of-institutional-research/Data/CDS/CDS2015_2016_web.pdf.

———. "Degree Requirements." Office of the Registrar, 2015. http://www.gonzaga.edu/Campus-resources/offices-and-services-A-Z/Registrar/Degree-Office/Undergraduate/DegreeRequirements.asp.

———. "Meet the Jesuits." 2016. https://www.gonzaga.edu/about/Mission/Jesuit-Community/Meet-the-Jesuits.asp.

———. "The Strategic Plan: Vision 2012." 2012. http://www.gonzaga.edu/Campus-Resources/TheStrategicPlan/default.asp.

———. "Undergraduate Student Body Diversity." Office of Institutional Research, 2015. https://www.gonzaga.edu/campus-Resources/Offices-and-Services-a-z/office-of-institutional-research/Data/F2015-Diversity-UG.pdf.

Gordon, Cynthia. "A(p)parent Play: Blending Frames and Reframing in Family Talk." *Language in Society* 37 (2008) 319–49.

Gray, Jessie. Focus group interview by Luisa J. Gallagher. Spokane, Washington, November 4, 2016. Transcript.

Bibliography

———. Personal interview by Luisa J. Gallagher. Spokane, Washington, November 12, 2016. Transcript.

Green, Sara. Interview by Luisa J. Gallagher. Focus Group Interview. Spokane, Washington, November 4, 2016. Transcript.

———. Personal interview by Luisa J. Gallagher. Spokane, Washington, November 11, 2016. Transcript.

Greenleaf, Robert K. *The Servant as Leader*. Cambridge, MA: Center for Applied Studies, 1970.

Hill, Peter C., and Kenneth I. Pargament. "Advances in the Conceptualization and Measurement of Religion and Spirituality." *American Psychologist* 58 (2003) 64–74.

Holcomb, Gary L., and Arthur J. Nonneman. "Faithful Change: Exploring and Assessing Faith Development in Christian Liberal Arts Undergraduates." In *Assessing Character Outcomes in College*, edited by Jon C. Dalton et al., 93–103. San Francisco: Jossey-Bass, 2004.

Hollinger, Dennis P. *Head, Heart and Hands: Bringing Together Christian Thought, Passion and Action*. Downers Grove: InterVarsity, 2005.

Hunt, James G., et al. "Leader Emotional Displays from Near and Far: The Implications of Close versus Distant Leadership for Leader Emotional Labor and Authenticity." In *Affect and Emotion: New Directions in Management Theory and Research*, edited by R. H. Humphrey, 41–63. Charlotte, NC: Information Age, 2008.

Ignatius of Loyola. *Ignatius of Loyola: Spiritual Exercises and Selected Works*. Translated by George E. Ganss. New York: Paulist, 1991.

Ignatius of Loyola, and Louis J. Puhl. *The Spiritual Exercises of St. Ignatius: Based on Studies in the Language of the Autograph*. Chicago: Loyola University Press, 1951.

International Commission on the Apostolate of Jesuit Education (ICAJE). "The Characteristics of Jesuit Education." In *The Jesuit Ratio Studiorum: 400th Anniversary Perspectives*, edited by Vincent J. Duminuco, 161–230. New York: Fordham University Press, 1986.

———. "Ignatian Pedagogy: A Practical Approach." In *The Jesuit Ratio Studiorum: 400th Anniversary Perspectives*, edited by Vincent J. Duminuco, 231–93. New York: Fordham University Press, 1993.

Jensen, Susan, and Fred Luthans. "Entrepreneurs as Authentic Leaders: Impact on Employees' Attitudes." *Leadership and Organization Development Journal* 8 (2006) 646–66.

Johnson, Katie. Personal interview by Luisa J. Gallagher. Spokane, Washington, November 4, 2016. Transcript.

Jones, Sidney. "Dr. Kent Hoffman Speaks at Gonzaga for Suffering and the Soul Week." *Gonzaga Bulletin*, October 4, 2016. http://www.gonzagabulletin.com/news/article_504ab750-8a59-11e6-a339-0fcfda037a9c.html.

Jones, Tristan. Focus group interview by Luisa J. Gallagher. Spokane, Washington, November 3, 2016. Transcript.

Bibliography

———. Personal interview by Luisa J. Gallagher. Spokane, Washington, November 11, 2016. Transcript.

Kegan, Robert. *In Over Our Heads: The Mental Demands of Modern Life.* Cambridge: Harvard University Press, 1994.

Kern, Josh. Focus group interview by Luisa J. Gallagher. Spokane, Washington, November 4, 2016. Transcript.

Kind, Jill. Focus group interview by Luisa J. Gallagher. Spokane, Washington, November 3, 2016. Transcript.

King, P. Marcia, and Patricia M. Magolda. "A Developmental Model of Intercultural Maturity." *Journal of College Student Development* 45 (2005) 571–92.

Kinnaman, David. "Most Twentysomethings Put Christianity on the Shelf Following Spiritually Active Teen Years." Barna Group, September 11, 2006. https://www.barna.com/research/most-twentysomethings-put-christianity-on-the-shelf-following-spiritually-active-teen-years/.

Koestenbaum, Peter. *Leadership: The Inner Side of Greatness; A Philosophy for Leaders.* Rev. ed. San Francisco: Jossey-Bass, 2002.

Komives, Susan R. "College Student Leadership Identity Development." In *Early Development and Leadership: Building the Next Generation of Leaders*, edited by Susan Elaine Murphy and Rebecca J. Reichard, 273–92. New York: Routledge, 2011.

———. "Spirituality and Leadership." *Journal of College and Character* 6 (2005). http://www.tandfonline.com/doi/pdf/10.2202/1940-1639.1466.

Komives, Susan R., and Wendy Wagner. *Leadership for a Better World: Understanding the Social Change Model of Leadership Development.* San Francisco: Jossey-Bass, 2009.

Komives, Susan R., Nance Lucas, and Timothy R. McMahon. *Exploring Leadership: For College Students Who Want to Make a Difference.* San Francisco: Jossey-Bass, 2013.

Komives, Susan R., et al. "Developing a Leadership Identity: A Grounded Theory." *Journal of College Student Development* 46 (2005) 593–611.

———. "Leadership Identity Model: Applications from a Grounded Theory." *Journal of College Student Development* 47 (2006) 401–18.

Lawrence-Turner, Jody. "Gonzaga University's Basketball Success Fuels Unprecedented Growth." *Spokesman Review*, November 24, 2013. http://www.spokesman.com/stories/2013/nov/24/gonzaga-universitys-basketball-success-fuels/.

Light, Richard J. *Making the Most of College: Students Speak Their Minds.* Cambridge: Harvard University Press, 2001.

Luthans, Fred, and Bruce J. Avolio. "Authentic Leadership: A Positive Developmental Approach." In *Positive Organizational Scholarship: Foundations of a New Discipline*, edited by Kim S. Cameron et al., 241–58. San Francisco: Berrett-Koehler, 2003.

Maddox, Randy L. "The Change of Affections: The Development, Dynamics, and Dethronement of John Wesley's 'Heart Religion.'" *Heart Religion in the Methodist Tradition and Related Movements*, edited by Richard Steele, 3–31. Metuchen, NJ: Scarecrow, 2001.

———. *Responsible Grace: John Wesley's Practical Theology*. Nashville: Abingdon, 1994.

Martin, James. *The Jesuit Guide to Almost Everything: A Spirituality for Real Life*. New York: HarperCollins, 2010.

May, Douglas R., et al. "Developing the Moral Component of Authentic Leadership." *Organizational Dynamics* 32 (2003) 247–60.

Merton, Thomas. *The Asian Journal of Thomas Merton*. Edited by Naomi Burton et al. New York: New Directions, 1973.

———. *Conjectures of a Guilty Bystander*. Garden City, NY: Doubleday, 1996.

———. *The Sign of Jonas*. Garden City, NY: Doubleday, 1956.

Nouwen, Henri J. M. *Reaching Out: The Three Movements of the Spiritual Life*. Garden City, NY: Doubleday, 1975.

———. *The Way of the Heart: Desert Spirituality and Contemporary Ministry*. San Francisco: Harper, 1981.

Nowacek, Rebecca, and Susan Mountin. "Reflection in Action: A Signature Ignatian Pedagogy for the 21st Century." In *Exploring More Signature Pedagogies: Approaches to Teaching Disciplinary Habits of Mind*, edited by Nancy L. Chick et al., 129–42. Sterling, VA: Stylus, 2012.

Outler, Albert C. "The Wesleyan Quadrilateral in John Wesley." *Wesleyan Theological Journal* 20 (1985) 7–18.

Palmer, Parker J. "Evoking the Spirit in Public Education." *Educational Leadership* 4 (1998) 6–11.

———. *Let Your Life Speak: Listening for the Voice of Vocation*. San Francisco: Jossey-Bass, 2000.

Parks, Sharon D. *Big Questions, Worthy Dreams: Mentoring Emerging Adults in Their Search for Meaning, Purpose and Faith*. San Francisco: Jossey-Bass, 2000.

Peterson, Eugene H. *A Long Obedience in the Same Direction: Discipleship in an Instant Society*. Downers Grove: InterVarsity, 2000.

Peus, Claudia, et al. "Authentic Leadership: An Empirical Test of Its Antecedents, Consequences, and Mediating Mechanisms." *Journal of Business Ethics* 3 (2012) 331–48.

Pile, Megan. Focus group interview by Luisa J. Gallagher. Spokane, Washington, November 3, 2016. Transcript.

Plowman, Stephanie. "Gonzaga History 1887–1895." Last modified March 2015. https://researchguides.gonzaga.edu/c.php?g=67718&p=1599164.

Raper, Mark. "Changing to Best Serve the Universal Mission." IHS Jesuit Asia Pacific Conference, May 19, 2012. http://sjapc.net/content/changing-best-serve-universal-mission.

Reed, Edward S. *The Necessity of Experience*. New Haven: Yale University Press, 1996.

Romney, A. Kimball., et al. "Culture as Consensus: A Theory of Culture and Informant Accuracy." *American Anthropologist* 88 (1986) 313–38.

Bibliography

Saad, Lydia. "In U.S., Rise in Religious 'Nones' Slows in 2012." Gallup, January 10, 2013. http://www.gallup.com/poll/159785/rise-religious-nones-slows-2012.aspx.

Shahabi, Leila, et al. "Correlates of Self-Perception of Spirituality in American Adults." *Annals of Behavioral Medicine* 24 (2002) 59–68.

Smith, Joy. Focus group interview by Luisa J. Gallagher. Spokane, Washington, November 3, 2016. Transcript.

———. Personal interview by Luisa J. Gallagher. Spokane, Washington, November 10, 2016. Transcript.

Spears, Larry C. "Character and Servant Leadership: Ten Characteristics of Effective, Caring Leaders." *Journal of Virtues and Leadership* 1 (2010) 25–30.

Stogdill, Ralph M. *Handbook of Leadership: A Survey of Theory and Research.* New York: Free Press, 1974.

Terry, Robert W. *Authentic Leadership: Courage in Action.* New York: Wiley, 1993.

Thorsen, Donald A. *The Wesleyan Quadrilateral: Scripture, Tradition, Reason and Experience as a Model of Evangelical Theology.* Grand Rapids: Zondervan, 1990.

Underhill, Evelyn. *Evelyn Underhill: Essential Writings.* Selected by Emilie Griffin. Modern Spiritual Masters Series. Maryknoll: Orbis, 2003.

Vygotsky, Lev S. *Mind in Society: The Development of Higher Psychological Processes.* Cambridge: Harvard University Press, 1978.

Walumbwa, Fred O., et al. "Authentic Leadership: Developing and Validation of a Theory-Based Measure." *Journal of Management* 34 (2008) 89–126.

Wenger, Etienne. *Communities of Practice: Learning, Meaning, and Identity.* Cambridge: Cambridge University Press, 1998.

Werhane, Patricia H., et al. "Social Constructivism, Mental Models, and Problems of Obedience." *Journal of Business Ethics* 100 (2011) 103–18.

Wesley, John. "Letter to Dr. Rutherforth." In vol. 8 of *The Works of the Rev. John Wesley.* New York: Harper, 1827.

———. "Sermon 16." In vol. 5 of *The Works of the Rev. John Wesley.* New York: Harper, 1830.

———. "Sermon 19: The Great Privilege of those that are Born of God." In vol. 1 of *Sermons on Several Occasions: By the Rev. John Wesley.* New York: Harper, 1831.

———. "Sermon 70: The Case of Reason Impartially Considered." In vol. 6 of *The Works of the Rev. John Wesley.* London: Mason, 1829.

White, Lloyd. Focus group interview by Luisa J. Gallagher. Spokane, Washington, November 3, 2016. Transcript.

———. Personal interview by Luisa J. Gallagher. Spokane, Washington, November 13, 2016. Transcript.

Wilhoit, James C., and John M. Dettoni, eds. *Nurture That Is Christian: Developmental Perspectives on Christian Education.* Grand Rapids: Baker, 1995.

Bibliography

Wilhoit, Jim C., et al. "Soul Projects: Class-Related Spiritual Practices in Higher Education." *Journal of Spiritual Formation and Soul Care* 2 (2009) 153–78.

Willard, Dallas. *Renovation of the Heart: Putting on the Character of Christ.* Colorado Springs: NavPress, 2002.

———. "Transformation of the Mind." *Spring Arbor University Journal*, Summer 2003.

Williams, Caleb. Focus group interview by Luisa J. Gallagher. Spokane, Washington, November 4, 2016. Transcript.

Wood, Ralph J., and Eddie Hebert. "The Relationship between Spiritual Meaning and Purpose and Drug and Alcohol Use among College Students." *American Journal of Health Studies* 20 (2005) 72–79.

Woodward, Dudley B., Jr., et al. "Leadership." *New Directions for Student Services* 92 (2000) 81–91.

Wuthnow, Robert. *After Heaven: Spirituality in America since the 1950s.* Berkeley: University of California Press, 1998.

Yukl, Gary A. *Leadership in Organizations.* Englewood Cliffs, NJ: Prentice Hall, 1994.

www.ingramcontent.com/pod-product-compliance
Lightning Source LLC
Chambersburg PA
CBHW051943160426
43198CB00013B/2275